A GUIDE TO

HARD TIMES

A GUIDE TO

HARD TIMES

SEAN SHEEHAN

WITH TONY BUZAN

Hodder & Stoughton

ISBN 0 340 77563 7

First published 2000
Impression number   10 9 8 7 6 5 4 3 2 1
Year   2005 2004 2003 2002 2001 2000

The 'Teach Yourself' name and logo are registered trade marks of
Hodder & Stoughton Ltd.

Cover photograph: BBC Worldwide
Illustrations: David Ashby
Mind Maps: Ann Jones

Typeset by Transet Limited, Coventry, England.
Printed in Great Britain for Hodder & Stoughton Educational, a division of
Hodder Headline Plc, 338 Euston Road, London NW1 3BH by Cox and Wyman Ltd,
Reading, Berks.

CONTENTS

You are now in the most important educational stage of your life, and are soon to take English Literature exams that may have a major impact on your future career and goals. As one A-level student put it: 'It's crunch time!'

At this crucial stage of your life the one thing you need even more than subject knowledge is the knowledge of *how* to remember, *how* to read faster, *how* to comprehend, *how* to study, *how* to take notes and *how* to organize your thoughts. You need to know how to *think*; you need a basic introduction on how to use that super bio-computer inside your head – your brain.

The next eight pages contain a goldmine of information on how you can achieve success both at school and in your A-level English literature exams, as well as in your professional or university career. These eight pages will give you skills that will enable you to be successful in *all* your academic pursuits. You will learn:

◆ How to recall more *while* you are learning.
◆ How to recall more *after* you have finished a class or a study period.
◆ How to use special techniques to improve your memory.
◆ How to use a revolutionary note-taking technique called Mind Maps that will double your memory and help you to write essays and answer exam questions.
◆ How to read everything faster while at the same time improving your comprehension and concentration.
◆ How to zap your revision!

How to understand, improve and master your memory of Literature Guides

Your memory really is like a muscle. Don't exercise it and it will grow weaker; *do* exercise it properly and it will grow incredibly more powerful. There are really only four main things you need to understand about your  memory in order, dramatically, to increase its power:

Recall during learning
– YOU MUST TAKE BREAKS!

When you are studying, your memory can concentrate, understand and recall well for between 20 and 45 minutes at a time. Then it *needs* a break. If you carry on for longer than this without one, your memory starts to break down. If you study for hours non-stop, you will remember only a fraction of what you have been trying to learn, and you will have wasted valuable revision time.

So, ideally, *study for less than an hour*, then take a five- to ten-minute break. During this break listen to music, go for a walk, do some exercise, or just daydream. (Daydreaming is a necessary brain-power booster – geniuses do it regularly.) During the break your brain will be sorting out what it has been learning and you will go back to your study with the new information safely stored and organized in your memory banks. Make *sure* you take breaks at regular intervals as you work through the *Literature Guides*.

Recall after learning
– SURFING THE WAVES OF YOUR MEMORY

What do you think begins to happen to your memory straight *after* you have finished learning something? Does it immediately start forgetting? No! Surprisingly, your brain actually *increases* its power and carries on remembering. For a short time after your study session, your brain integrates the information, making a more complete picture of everything it has just learnt. Only then does the rapid decline in memory begin, as much as 80 per cent of what you have learnt can be forgotten in a day.

However, if you catch the top of the wave of your memory, and briefly review what you have been revising at the correct time, the memory is stamped in far more strongly, and stays at the crest of the wave for a much longer time. To maximize your brain's power to remember, take a few minutes and use a Mind Map to review what you have learnt at the end of a day. Then review it at the end of a week, again at the end of a month, and finally a week before the exams. That way you'll surf-ride your memory wave all the way to your exam, success and beyond!

The memory principle of association

The muscle of your memory becomes stronger when it can **associate** – when it can link things together.

Think about your best friend, and all the things your mind *automatically* links with that person. Think about your favourite hobby, and all the associations your mind has when you think about (remember!) that hobby.

When you are studying, use this memory principle to make associations between the elements in your subjects, and to thus improve both your memory and your chances of success.

The memory principle of imagination

The muscle of your memory will improve significantly if you can produce big images in your mind. Rather than just memorizing the name of a character, imagine that character of the novel or play as if you were a video producer filming that person's life. The same goes for images in poetry.

In *all* your subjects use the **imagination** memory principle.

Throughout this *Literature Guide* you will find special association and imagination techniques (called mnemonics after the Greek goddess Mnemosyne) that will make it much easier for you to remember the topic being discussed. Look out for them!

Your new success formula: Mind Maps®

You have noticed that when people go on holidays, or travel, they take maps. Why? To give them a general picture of where they are going, to help them locate places of special interest and importance, to help them find things more easily, and to help them remember distances and locations, etc.

It is exactly the same with your mind and with study. If you have a 'map of the territory' of what you have to learn, then everything is easier. In learning and study, the Mind Map is that special tool.

As well as helping you with all areas of study, the Mind Map actually *mirrors the way your brain works.* Your Mind Maps can be used for taking notes from your study books, for taking notes in class, for preparing your homework, for presenting your homework, for reviewing your tests, for checking your and your friends' knowledge in any subject, and for *helping you understand anything you learn.* Mind Maps are especially useful in English literature, as they allow you to map out the whole territory of a novel, play or poem, giving you an 'at-a-glance' snapshot of all the key information you need to know.

The Mind Maps in the *Literature Guide* use, throughout, **imagination** and **association**. As such, they automatically strengthen your memory muscle every time you use them. Throughout this guide you will find Mind Maps that summarize the most important areas of the English Literature guide you are studying. Study these Mind Maps, add some colour, personalize them, and then have a go at making your own Mind Maps of the work you are studying – you will remember them far better! Put them on your walls and in your files for a quick and easy review. Mind Maps are fast, efficient, effective and, importantly, *fun* to do!

HOW TO DRAW A MIND MAP

1 Start in the middle of the page with the page turned sideways. This gives your brain more radiant freedom for its thoughts.

2 Always start by drawing a picture or symbol of the novel or its title. Why? Because *a picture is worth a thousand words to your brain.* Try to use at least three colours, as colour helps your memory even more.

3 Let your thoughts flow, and write or draw your ideas on coloured branching lines connected to your central image. The key symbols and words are the headings for your topic. The Mind Map at the top of the next page shows you how to start.

4 Next, add facts and ideas by drawing more, smaller, branches on to the appropriate main branches, just like a tree.

5 Always print your word clearly on its line. Use only one word per line.

6 To link ideas and thoughts on different branches, use arrows, colours, underlining and boxes.

HOW TO READ A MIND MAP

1 Begin in the centre, the focus of your novel, play or poem.

2 The words/images attached to the centre are like chapter headings; read them next.

3 Always read out from the centre, in every direction (even on the left-hand side, where you will read from right to left, instead of the usual left to right).

USING MIND MAPS

Mind Maps are a versatile tool – use them for taking notes in class or from books, for solving problems, for brainstorming with friends, and for reviewing and revising for exams – their uses are infinite! You will find them invaluable for planning essays for coursework and exams. Number your main branches in the order in which you want to use them and off you go – the main headings for your essay are done and all your ideas are logically organized!

Super speed reading and study

What do you think happens to your comprehension as your reading speed rises? 'It goes down!' Wrong! It seems incredible, but it has been proved – the faster you read, the more you comprehend and remember!

So here are some tips to help you to practise reading faster – you'll cover the ground much more quickly, remember more, *and* have more time for revision and leisure activities!

SUPER SPEED READING

1 First read the whole text (whether it's a lengthy book or an exam paper) very quickly, to give your brain an overall idea of what's ahead and get it working.
(It's like sending out a scout to look at the territory you have to cover – it's much easier when you know what to expect!) Then read the text again for more detailed information.
2 Have the text a reasonable distance away from your eyes. In this way your eye/brain system will be able to see more at a glance, and will naturally begin to read faster.
3 Take in groups of words at a time. Rather than reading 'slowly and carefully' read faster, more enthusiastically. Your comprehension will rocket!
4 Take in phrases rather than single words while you read.
5 Use a guide. Your eyes are designed to follow movement, so a thin pencil underneath the lines you are reading, moved smoothly along, will 'pull' your eyes to faster speeds.

HOW TO MAKE STUDY EASY FOR YOUR BRAIN

When you are going somewhere, is it easier to know beforehand where you are going, or not? Obviously it is easier if you *do* know. It is the same for your brain and a book. When you get a new book, there are seven things you can do to help your brain get to 'know the territory' faster:

1 Scan through the whole book in less than 20 minutes, as you would do if you were in a shop thinking whether or not to buy it. This gives your brain *control*.

2 Think about what you already know about the subject. You'll often find out it's a lot more than you thought. A good way of doing this is to do a quick Mind Map on *everything you know* after you have skimmed through it.

3 Ask who, what, why, where, when and how questions about what is in the book. Questions help your brain 'fish' the knowledge out.

4 Ask your friends what they know about the subject. This helps them review the knowledge in their own brains, and helps your brain get new knowledge about what you are studying.

5 Have another quick speed read through the book, this time looking for any diagrams, pictures and illustrations, and also at the beginnings and ends of chapters. Most information is contained in the beginnings and ends.

6 If you come across any difficult parts in your book, mark them and *move on*. Your brain *will* be able to solve the problems when you come back to them a bit later. Much like saving the difficult bits of a jigsaw puzzle for later. When you have finished the book, quickly review it one more time and then discuss it with friends. This will lodge it permanently in your memory banks.

7 Build up a Mind Map as you study the book. This helps your brain to organize and hold (remember!) information as you study.

Helpful hints for exam revision

◆ To avoid **exam panic** cram at the *start* of your course, not the end. It takes the same amount of time, so you may as well use it where it is best placed!

◆ Use Mind Maps throughout your course, and build a Master Mind Map for each subject – a giant Mind Map that summarizes everything you know about the subject.

◆ Use memory techniques such as mnemonics (verses or systems for remembering things like dates and events or lists).

◆ Get together with one or two friends to revise, compare Mind Maps, and discuss topics.

AND FINALLY ...

◆ *Have fun while you learn* – studies show that those people who enjoy what they are doing understand and remember it more, and generally do better.

◆ *Use your teachers* as resource centres. Ask them for help with specific topics and with more general advice on how you can improve your all-round performance.

◆ *Personalize your* **Literature Revision Guide** by underlining and highlighting, by adding notes and pictures. Allow your brain to have a conversation with it!

Your *amazing brain and its amazing cells*

Your brain is like a super, *super*, *SUPER* computer. The world's best computers have only a few thousand or hundred thousand computer chips. Your brain has 'computer chips' too, and they are called brain cells. Unlike the computer, you do not have only a few thousand computer chips – the number of brain cells in your head is a *million MILLION*!! This means you are a genius just waiting to discover yourself! All you have to do is learn how to get those brain cells working together, and you'll not only become more smart, you'll have more free time to pursue your other fun activities.

The more you understand your amazing brain the more it will repay and amaze you!

Apply its power to this *Literature Guide*!

(Tony Buzan)

HOW TO USE THIS GUIDE R¿

This guide assumes that you have already read *Hard Times*, although you could read 'Context' and 'The story of *Hard Times*' first. It is best to use the guide alongside the novel. You could read the 'Characterization' and 'Themes' sections without referring to the novel, but you will get more out of these if you do.

The sections

The 'Commentary' section can be used in a number of ways. One way is to read a chapter of the novel, and then read the relevant commentary. Keep on until you come to a test section, test yourself – then have a break! Alternatively, read the Commentary for a chapter, then read that chapter in the novel, then go back to the Commentary. See what works best for you.

'Critical approaches' sums up the main critical views and interpretations of the novel. Your own response is important, but be aware of these approaches too.

'How to get an "A" in English Literature' gives valuable advice on what to look for in a text, and what skills you need to develop in order to achieve your personal best.

'The exam essay' is a useful 'night before' reminder of how to tackle exam questions, though it will help you more if you also look at it much earlier in the year. 'Model answer' gives an example A-grade essay and the Mind Map and plan used to write it.

The questions

Whenever you come across a question in the guide with a star ✪ in front of it, think about it for a moment. You could make a Mini Mind Map or a few notes to focus your mind.
There is not usually a 'right' answer to these: it is important for you to develop your own opinions if you want to get an 'A'.
The 'Test' sections are designed to take you about 15–20 minutes each – time well spent. Take a short break after each one.

KEY TO ICONS

Themes

A **theme** is an idea explored by an author. Whenever a theme is dealt with in the guide, the appropriate icon is used. This means you can find where a theme is mentioned just by flicking through the book. Go on – try it now!

Reason and
imagination

Goodness

Parents

Marriage

Capitalism

Social class

 LANGUAGE, STYLE AND STRUCTURE

This heading and icon are used in the Commentary wherever there is a special section on the author's choice of words and imagery, and the overall plot structure.

Dickens' life

Charles Dickens was born in 1812 into a large lower-middle-class family. However, because of money problems he was sent to work in a London blacking factory at the age of 12. This deeply unhappy experience only came to an end when his father insisted that the boy receive an education. Many Dickens novels feature inadequate parents and unfortunate children.

Dickens went on to become a news reporter, and wrote short stories for magazines before emerging as a successful novelist. In 1849 he launched his own weekly magazine, *Household Words*, and in 1854 he began work on a serial to boost sales. He divided his plot into monthly parts which could later be subdivided for weekly publication. He considered various titles (see page 87) before settling on *Hard Times*.

Shortly after starting the work Dickens set off to the industrial north of England to observe a weavers' strike then in its fourth month. The employers had organized a lockout and a bitter stand-off resulted. Dickens' attendance at a workers' meeting seems to have reinforced his opinion that strikers had genuine complaints but were manipulated by self-elected leaders who did not have the workers' welfare at heart.

After returning, Dickens had two months before the first instalment was due. He spoke in letters of the 'perpetual difficulty' arising from the need for 'compression and close condensation'. He worked fast, but at times was only keeping two weeks ahead of publication. He finished writing in France, where he had rented a house – six months after he had begun the project.

Dickens achieved public fame and although he remained married to Catherine Hogarth for over twenty years he carried on a secret affair with an actress, Ellen Terry, for many years. He finally separated from his wife in 1858. His workaholic lifestyle took its toll on his health and he died at the age of 58 in 1870.

Historical and social context

Dickens grew up in the throes of Britain's industrial revolution and he was not blind to the social and political turmoil caused by the tremendous and far-reaching economic changes. *Hard Times* was dedicated to his acquaintance Thomas Carlyle, a writer and social critic who was as alarmed as Dickens over the way industrialization and the relentless pursuit of profit were reducing workers to the level of machine parts. Bounderby refers to his workers as mere *Hands*.

Although trade unions were campaigning for better working conditions Dickens had little more faith in the trade union leaders than in the MPs who were in a position to enact new laws. In *Hard Times*, Gradgrind becomes an MP and Dickens suggests that his work consists of shuffling papers around and compiling reports that always fail to get to the heart of the social problems they are supposed to address.

The dismay Dickens felt at the growing divisions in society was heightened by his lack of faith in institutions. He looked to people, not organizations, for change. His view was that individuals needed to feel differently about how they lived and worked with each other. Although his attack on capitalism was penetrating and radical, he hoped for a revolution of the heart rather than a revolution on the streets. This is the sentiment behind the final sentence of *Hard Times*.

Dickens much admired Elizabeth Gaskell (1810–65), a novelist who shared his concern with the social impact of industrialization. It is worth reading her *North and South*, serialized in *Household Words* in 1854–5: it tackles some of the same themes as *Hard Times*, but in a very different way. Another contemporary 'social issue' novel worth reading is Robert Tressell's *The Ragged Trousered Philanthropist*.

Book the first: Sowing

The story begins in a classroom in the industrial town of
Coketown, with the children being lectured by **Gradgrind** on
the importance of facts, the need for a **rational** outlook and the
worthlessness of the **imagination**. When Gradgrind finds his
own children **Louisa** and **Tom** peeping into a travelling **circus**
he is convinced by his friend **Bounderby**, a Coketown factory
owner and banker, that a circus child, **Sissy Jupe**, should be
removed from his school.

After Gradgrind finds that Sissy's father has abandoned her he
determines instead to bring her into his family and rear her on
the same strict principles he applies to his own children.
Bounderby, who thinks this is a foolish idea, has his eyes on
the young Louisa as a future wife despite a thirty-year
difference in their ages. When she is 18 Bounderby proposes
the marriage to Gradgrind and the dispirited Louisa resigns
herself to being Mrs Bounderby.

Mrs Sparsit, Bounderby's housekeeper, takes up residence
above his bank in Coketown while the Bounderbys move to
their new home in the country. **Bitzer**, a product of Gradgrind's
educational philosophy, now works in Bounderby's bank.

Bounderby receives a visit from **Stephen Blackpool**, a worker
in his factory, who seeks advice on his hopeless marriage to an
alcoholic who has left him but who periodically returns to
plague him. Stephen seeks a divorce so that he can marry
Rachel, a fellow worker whom he has known for years.
Bounderby self-righteously informs him that nothing can be
done by someone who cannot afford the substantial costs then
involved in gaining a divorce. On his way home Stephen meets
an old woman, **Mrs Pegler**, who likes to know how Bounderby
is doing.

Book the second: Reaping

Louisa and Bounderby are visited by **James Harthouse**, an idle
gentleman of 35 who has a letter of introduction from

Gradgrind, who by now is a member of parliament. Harthouse is interested in making a career in politics. Tom Gradgrind by now is working in Bounderby's bank but he has run up gambling debts. Harthouse learns from Tom what he already suspects, namely that Louisa has no love for her husband, and resolves to seduce her.

Stephen Blackpool finds himself **ostracized** at work because he promised Rachel not to join a trade union and **Slackbridge** whips up feeling against him. Although Rachel regrets the promise, Stephen feels honour-bound to keep it and accepts his fate with equanimity. Bounderby summons Stephen, hoping he now has an unpaid spy working for him, but when Stephen defends his fellow workers and points out the injustice of their conditions Bounderby **sacks him** in a rage.

Louisa visits Stephen to offer sympathy and money, but Tom, who accompanies her, seizes a chance to shift the blame for his plan to **rob the bank** onto the unsuspecting Stephen. Just before Stephen leaves Coketown to find work elsewhere, Tom robs the bank and suspicion falls on Stephen as he intended. The mysterious old woman, Mrs Pegler, is also suspected of involvement in the robbery.

Mrs Sparsit, driven by jealousy, **spies on Louisa** and Harthouse, convinced that they will embark on an affair when Bounderby is away in London. She hides in the shrubbery when Harthouse does indeed propose an affair to Louisa, but is wrong-footed when Louisa flees to her father's house and confronts him with the truth of her **loveless marriage** and the emotional poverty of her upbringing.

Book the third: Garnering

Gradgrind is stunned when he realizes his share of the responsibility for Louisa's unhappiness, while she is comforted by Sissy, who has grown into a mature woman. **Sissy** visits the puzzled Harthouse and persuades him to leave Coketown and never return. Meanwhile Mrs Sparsit has travelled to London to inform Bounderby of what she thinks has happened, only to find out the truth when they return to Coketown. Bounderby gives Louisa an **ultimatum** to either return home or sever their marriage and Louisa has no doubts about staying with her father and Sissy.

Attention shifts to the search for **Stephen** but Rachel insists on his innocence and writes to him asking him to come back and prove it. She is mystified by his failure to return, although a smaller mystery is solved when Mrs Sparsit captures poor **Mrs Pegler** and brings her back to Bounderby's house. The woman turns out to be Bounderby's mother, a loving parent – not at all as Bounderby has described her.

The following Sunday Sissy and Rachel discover a deserted **mine shaft** into which Stephen has fallen while rushing back to Coketown. He is rescued but before he dies from his injuries he alerts Gradgrind to Tom's involvement in the bank robbery. Sissy overhears and urges Tom to escape and take refuge in Sleary's travelling circus. Gradgrind, Louisa and Sissy go to meet him and arrange his escape, but **Bitzer** has followed Gradgrind and turns up unexpectedly to apprehend Tom.

Sleary and his circus friends arrange the escape from the clutches of Bitzer and Tom flees to America, never to return. The novel concludes with a glimpse into a future where Gradgrind has abandoned politics, Sissy is happily married with children, and where Louisa does not remarry but becomes a happier and more contented woman.

The Mini Mind Map above summarizes the main characters in *Hard Times*. When you have read this section, look at the full Mind Map on p. 13, then make a copy of the Mini Mind Map and try to add to it from memory.

Dickens is famous for the amazing variety of characters that people his books: a hundred characters in one novel is not unusual for him. *Hard Times*, constrained by the fact that the story was serialized fortnightly, has only a handful of main characters and about twenty in total. This helps to explain why each character is developed in some depth and is significant in a number of ways.

A general feature of Dickens' **characterization** (the way characters are presented) is the use of **caricature** (the exaggeration and simplification of character traits) and this is readily apparent in *Hard Times* from the first chapter. However, the elements of caricature in this novel always serve a purpose and relate to the themes and concerns that the author is exploring.

It is also important to remember that, while the characterization may involve comic or absurd exaggeration, it does not follow that the characters themselves are any less 'real' and convincing because of the method used to bring them to life in a work of fiction. At the same time, Dickens' priority is not in-depth psychological analysis. This is one way of approaching character, but not the only way. Dickens is more interested in setting up character types than in creating unique personalities such as, say, Hamlet or Othello. He does so with a rich sense of the theatrical.

❂ Think of a psychologically complex character from another text you are studying. How does its author's method of characterization differ from that of *Hard Times*?

Remember also that caricature is not the last word on characterization in *Hard Times* because the author is also interested in the psychology of the individual and Dickens is quite capable of juggling with different styles of characterization. An example of this is found in Gradgrind himself.

Gradgrind

Thomas Gradgrind, retired merchant and father to Louisa, Tom and three younger children, begins as a caricature and ends as a very human and sympathetic character. Examples of caricature using his personal appearance and demeanour are plentiful in the first two chapters. Look, too, at the description of his home, Stone Lodge, in the third chapter. His role here as the representative of an unyielding ideology that elevates facts and reason at the expense of personal creativity and the imagination is expressed through a multitude of **metaphors** (images describing things as if they were something else).

Gradgrind is also a parent of young children and it is in the personal, private world of his family life that the caricature comes down to earth. His inflexible and narrow understanding of human development is based on 'utilitarianism', which discards anything that cannot be said to be strictly useful. It produces two very unhappy children and the novel reveals the full human cost of his misguided though well-meaning intention to conduct his family life strictly in accordance with his rationalistic philosophy.

As the story draws to a close, Gradgrind becomes a broken and disillusioned man who abandons his political career but becomes a wiser and better person. Gradgrind is the spokesperson of the rationalistic, utilitarian doctrine and his failure can be interpreted as the symbolic failure of this system. He can also be seen as a parent who spends too little time with his wife and children, thinking professional life more important than family life, and who finds out the hard way what is really important in life. The scenes in Book 3, Chapters 7 and 8, where he meets his son and is then confronted by Bitzer, skilfully weave the collapse of Gradgrind the parent and Gradgrind the educationist.

Bounderby

In an important respect Bounderby is characterized as the equivalent in the economic sphere of Gradgrind's role in the educational arena. Just as Gradgrind reduces the complex process of learning and growing up to a simplistic formula, Bounderby the factory owner and banker applies a reductionist approach to his employees. The method of characterization is also similar, employing a host of metaphors to suggest character, and where Gradgrind was *square* Bounderby is *puffed* and *inflated*.

The differences between the two men are also important and the characterization of Bounderby, unlike that of Gradgrind, does not change. To the very end, the man who is a *bully of humility* remains linked with images of unyielding coarseness and cruelty and, even after his death, his will leaves a legacy of conflict and chicanery. The man himself, again unlike Gradgrind, does not change, and the exposure of his lie about his family background does nothing to dent his bullying, violent nature.

It is worth stressing just how ugly Bounderby is as a human being because he should not be viewed merely as a caricature of the bloated capitalist who hypocritically exploits his employees. On the human level, he is a very unpleasant individual whose cruel treatment of his own mother, as revealed in Book 3, Chapter 5, is quite in character with the man who heartlessly told the young Sissy, in Book 1, Chapter 6, about her father's disappearance.

Louisa

Louisa is the most psychologically rounded character in the novel and her characterization refutes the criticism that in *Hard Times* Dickens reduces characters to mere types. The reader follows her development from childhood onwards and the psychological astuteness with which she is portrayed complements the more philosophical treatment of social, political and educational ideas in the novel.

Louisa's spirited and imaginative nature is noted from her first appearance in Book 1, Chapter 3, and her natural repulsion towards Bounderby in the following chapter. The story of her growing up through adolescence into a young woman reveals the anguish she feels but cannot fully comprehend because of her age, limited experience and, crucially, emotional deprivation. Key moments in her life include the question of her marriage to Bounderby, in Book 1, Chapters 14 and 15, and her final encounter with Harthouse in Book 2, Chapter 12.

Louisa's capacity for love and need for affection are channelled into her concern for Tom, and Harthouse represents a very real temptation. Her fraught conversation with her father at the end of the second book carries tremendous emotional power even though the language may not strike us as realistic. Her recovery with the help of Sissy is touching but never sentimental and Dickens does not provide a fairytale happy ending for her in the last chapter of the novel.

Tom Gradgrind $R\ell$

The characterization of Tom Gradgrind is similar to that of Louisa in that he is also portrayed as a victim of a dysfunctional family. Unlike his sister, he lacks imagination and empathy for others and this crucial difference in their natures is registered in Book 1, Chapter 8. Louisa's imaginative capacity as a child expresses itself as she gazes into the fire. Tom himself notes, *You seem to find more to look at in it than ever I could find.* He suffers, like his sister, from a lack of the emotional security that his parents should have provided, but it affects his character in a different way and he becomes the sullen reprobate who exploits his sister and Stephen Blackpool.

Sissy Jupe $R\ell$

Sissy's symbolic importance cannot be dissociated from her circus background, for unlike Louisa and Tom she was nurtured by a warm and loving family environment in early childhood. As a young child she was influenced by values that oppose, and finally triumph over, those of Gradgrind and

Bounderby. This is first registered in the second chapter of the book and becomes the keynote of her characterization.

Her role is symbolic, though perhaps no more so than Louisa's or Tom's, and there are many fine moments in the story where her positive values are realized in a very human and psychologically convincing manner. See, for example, the very end of Book 1, Chapter 15, where Sissy and Louisa exchange looks upon the announcement of Louisa's engagement to Bounderby.

Sissy's role in the events occupying the last book of the novel is paramount and she plays a crucial part in relations between Louisa, Rachel, Harthouse and Tom. She is able to empathize with Louisa and Rachel, offering friendship and solidarity, but she is also capable of dealing with Harthouse and her pragmatism is demonstrated more than once in the dramatic events that bring the story to an end. At a symbolic level this is tremendously important because it helps break down what has been seen as a simplistic opposition between reason and imagination in the novel. Her practical skills and powers of organization are eminently rational but they are motivated by values and aspirations that have nothing in common with the mercantile ethics that Gradgrind once championed and which Bounderby personifies.

Bitzer, Mrs Sparsit, Harthouse

Bitzer, Mrs Sparsit and Harthouse are very different characters in their own right but all three are characterized as people who lack a basic humanitarian instinct. They come from different social classes but they share a fundamental inability to love and form relationships based on trust and decency. This, for Dickens, is the moral litmus paper that forms the basis for judging people. Bitzer, Mrs Sparsit and Harthouse are all realized as individuals with their own very different personalities but they are also characterized as products of their society, embodying particular values.

Bitzer, in terms of his character in childhood and his later behaviour as an adult, makes a dramatic contrast with Sissy. His attitude to life is shaped by his schooling and there is a rich irony in the way he later applies what Gradgrind taught him in order to arrest Tom Gradgrind. He undergoes no change or development in his personality and this is very deliberate on the part of Dickens because the author wants to stress Bitzer's inability to respond to people and situations on a human level.

Mrs Sparsit's character matches the uncongenial sound of her name. She is mean-spirited to the very core of her being, and ranks alongside Bounderby as one of the two most unpleasant characters in the world of *Hard Times*. Her unpleasantness is psychologically interesting and, although Dickens does not delve deeply into her mind, there is something very morbid about the enjoyment she takes in following the break-up of the marriage between Louisa and Bounderby.

Harthouse is not unpleasant in the way that Bitzer and Mrs Sparsit are but he is equally deficient as a human being. He is intelligent but so lacks a moral centre that out of mere boredom he is happy to connive at the break-up of Louisa's marriage. It is his complete lack of principles that makes him so uncaring.

Stephen Blackpool and Rachel R^{ℓ}

Stephen Blackpool plays an important part in the plot of the novel but his characterization has some weaknesses. His passive suffering strikes many readers as unconvincing and his reason for not joining with his fellow workers in a trade union is especially so. His role seems to be largely symbolic, and while this is also true of Rachel her characterization seems stronger. This may be due to the positive values and virtues she embodies, while Stephen is rendered more as a passive victim. Rachel comes across as a warm person, with a degree of self-awareness and self-confidence that is lacking in Stephen.

❂ How convincing do you find these two characters? If your response is a negative one, try to find examples of their behaviour that support how you feel about them.

Minor characters R^{ℓ}

The minor characters in the novel fulfil various functions and they range from the teacher M'Choakumchild, whose significance is represented purely by his wonderful name, to more important figures like Sleary. The head of the circus, Sleary plays an important part in the culminating events of the story and in Book 3, Chapter 8 delivers a homily to Gradgrind that sums up the moral force that the circus symbolically represents.

Mrs Gradgrind plays a very minor role but this, paradoxically, is her significance. She is an inadequate parent to Louisa and Tom but this is partly because her husband has marginalized her to the point where her existence is hardly acknowledged. The characterization of Slackbridge, the union man, is probably the weakest in the novel and a chief reason for this is his use of language which strikes many readers and critics as unsatisfactory and unrealistic. ✪ Find an example of Slackbridge's language that might be described as unconvincing.

Over to You

? Take a blank sheet of paper and draw a set of icons for the main characters, perhaps using items you associate with them or their names. You may prefer to make your own drawings of them, instead of using icons. Spread them across the page, label them with key words to describe them, scenes that reveal their character, and perhaps a quotation from the text that describes them or how they see themselves and how you see them.

Now that you've brushed up on the characters, take a break before looking at the themes.

A **theme** is an idea which runs through a work and which is explored and developed along the way. The Mini Mind Map above shows the main themes of *Hard Times*. Test yourself by copying it and then trying to add to it before comparing your results with the version on p. 19.

Dickens had to sit down and work out a plan for the weekly serialization of *Hard Times* but he did not plan themes for his novel in the same way. The book succeeds as a whole through the power of the author's vision of society and his ability to communicate this vision through language and character, and there is something necessarily artificial about separating out and identifying a set of themes. The exercise of identifying and tracing the themes below is only worthwhile if it increases our understanding and appreciation of the way they overlap and reinforce each other, working together to produce a penetrating and radical criticism of Victorian society.

Reason and imagination

Reason, as represented by Gradgrind in his lecture to the schoolchildren in the opening chapters, and imagination, as represented by the world of the circus, have been identified as a binary opposition that runs thematically through the heart of the novel. Some critics have seen the handling of this theme as a central weakness of *Hard Times*. They claim that it is dealt with in a simplistic way (see p. 88).

It can be argued, on the other hand, that the theme is a rich one which is handled with subtlety. Gradgrind's educational philosophy is exaggerated in the classroom scenes but its effect on his own children, and the way it makes them unable to cope with their adult lives, is no **parody** (humorous exaggeration). The consequences of Gradgrind's misguided but well-intentioned principles come across with a remarkable and convincing degree of seriousness.

Bitzer is another product of a system that prioritizes reason at the expense of other human characteristics. The imagination is represented by the world of the circus and, while it might seem an inadequate metaphor to counter the power of a dogmatic and narrow-minded reason, is more fully realized in the figure of Sissy Jupe. Any simple dichotomy that turns reason and imagination into polar opposites, as if one must choose *either* reason *or* imagination, is undermined by having Sissy grow up in both worlds and emerge as a model of maturity. See p. 94, where this topic is dealt with as an essay question.

Goodness

Dickens certainly believes that, at a fundamental level, some people have more goodness than others, and such an idea may not in itself seem difficult to accept. In *Hard Times* we have people like Sissy and Rachel, paragons of goodness, and we also have some very nasty people like Bounderby and Mrs Sparsit, who are driven by malice and lack any redeeming features. This can create the impression that Dickens simplifies the nature of good and evil, peopling his novel with unrealistic characters who are absolutely good or absolutely bad. This is not the case, however, because *Hard Times* does explore the nature of goodness; even Stephen Blackpool finds himself seriously tempted by the opportunity of allowing his wife to poison herself.

Gradgrind, from the outset of the book, is well-intentioned and thinks he is doing what is good for his children. His son Tom is largely responsible for the death of another human being but he is not evil. Goodness, for Dickens, is something that comes from the heart and can be nurtured. Bitzer lacks goodness and may well become as thoroughly unpleasant an adult, in his own way, as Bounderby. It is relevant to imagine the way differences between his childhood experiences and those of someone like Sissy or Rachel may have contributed to this. ❂ What might have been lacking in Bitzer's childhood that would help account for his failings?

The nature of goodness is related to the theme of reason and imagination, for Dickens explores the connections between the capacity to love and feel compassion for others with the cultivation of the imagination.

Parents

Inadequate parenting, a familiar theme in many of Dickens' novels, is explored in *Hard Times* and related to other themes in the novel. The unhappy childhood of Louisa and Tom is a result of their father's misguided attempts to educate and bring them up under a rigid and inadequate philosophy. Mrs Gradgrind is an inept mother whose weak personality allows her husband to impose his ideas on their children's upbringing. Sissy, in Book 1, Chapter 7, has happy memories of her childhood with her father but, however well-intentioned his motives, she is deserted by him.

The theme receives an **ironic** twist (the opposite of what might be expected) in Bounderby's fiction of his own childhood. The only unblemished picture of good parenting emerges very briefly in the third from last paragraph of the novel. Here, Sissy's future role as a parent is guided by the concern that her children *should have a childhood of the mind no less than a childhood of the body*. Apart from Sissy's own memories of reading to her father, this positive ideal of parenting remains painfully and tantalizingly absent from *Hard Times*.

Book 2, Chapter 9, where Louisa remembers her miserable childhood, connects the theme of parents with that of reason and imagination. The two themes clearly overlap towards the end of the novel when Gradgrind realizes that his principles of reason and self-interest are less important than family loyalty. Thus he acts to protect his son Tom even though Tom is indirectly responsible for the death of Stephen Blackpool, conspiring with the circus to help Tom escape.

Marriage

Stephen Blackpool's marriage and the marriage of Bounderby and Louisa are prominent examples of failed marriages. The Gradgrind marriage is less dramatic, but it has its own significance. Part of the emotional poverty of their children's life is the absence for Louisa and Tom of any adequate model of a warm and loving relationship. The *pain somewhere in the room* that the dying Mrs Gradgrind speaks of in Book 2, Chapter 9 relates not only to the inadequacies of her husband's philosophy but also to the dismal failure of their married life in providing fulfilment for themselves and their children. The theme of marriage goes well beyond the particular historical context and the circumstances that made divorce practically impossible for the majority of people at the time Dickens was writing. The concern with love and the need for relationships based on mutual affection and compassion, seen by Dickens as the wellspring of personal happiness, accounts for the way marriages are looked at in the novel.

Capitalism

The profound economic, social and political changes brought about by the rise of industrial capitalism, an economic system based upon private capital and profit-making, constitute a major theme in the novel. Book 1, Chapter 5 is pointedly entitled 'The Key-Note', and its seventh paragraph makes an explicit connection between the industrial world of Coketown and the family life of the Gradgrinds. The power of the novel is built on the way the personal and the political are interwoven. For example, similarities are drawn between Bounderby's treatment of his employees and Gradgrind's treatment of his children.

At the end of the novel Dickens returns to this inter-relationship between the way people treat one another on a personal level and the logic of the free market. In Book 3, Chapter 8, this time pointedly entitled 'Philosophical', Bitzer's behaviour is related to capitalist values of competitive self-interest and Sleary suggests to Gradgrind what an alternative, non-capitalist ethics would be like.

Social class

Each character in the novel is placed within a particular social class and the divisions and conflicts between these classes lead to what Stephen Blackpool calls a *muddle*. The conflict between the working class and the class that employs them is at the heart of Coketown life, and Book 2, Chapter 5, where Stephen is dismissed by Bounderby, focuses explicitly on this theme.

The personally divisive nature of class distinctions is a theme that runs through the novel as a whole. It first emerges in the encounter between Bounderby and the circus people in Book 1, Chapter 6. The following chapter, with the introduction of Mrs Sparsit and her pretensions to gentility, adds another layer to the class structure of the world of *Hard Times*. Bounderby is obsessed with social class and invents the fiction of his deprived social origins to support his inverted snobbery.

On a positive note, Louisa makes a decision to visit Stephen after he has been dismissed and consciously crosses the social divide that has created separate worlds for them up until then.

Over to You again

?   Take a sheet of paper and draw the theme icons across it. Think about how they connect and overlap. For example, the social classes that Bounderby and Stephen Blackpool belong to are the result of the capitalist economic system. Draw lines to link the themes and label them with keywords to show the connections.

The language, style and structure of *Hard Times* are remarkably interconnected and, although they are being looked at separately here, think about how they relate to and influence each other.

Language

Dickens wrote the novel for serialization in a weekly magazine and this necessitated a highly condensed style of writing. Key ideas and aspects of character are realized through **metaphors** and **images**, using words in an imaginative way that is not literally true, and many examples can be found in the novel's opening chapter (see p. 26). The description of Bounderby's front door, in Book 1, Chapter 12, or the description of Coketown in the earlier Chapter 10, serve as examples of the way in which **signifiers**, the verbal signs, merge with the **signified**, the meaning which the sign represents. The *stunted and crooked shapes* of the working-class houses in Coketown identify the poverty and deprivation of those who live within the houses in the same way that Bounderby's nameplate on his door, *a brazen full-stop*, identifies the personality of the resident.

A belief in the identification of the signifier and the signified (as opposed to Dickens' use of this as a literary technique) is also at the heart of Gradgrind's and Bounderby's mental outlooks. Bitzer's definition of a horse is deemed correct because of the assumption that the words, signifiers like *quadruped* and *graminivorous*, represent the totality of the meaning of a horse, the signified. Consequently, Sissy is now expected to *know what a horse is.*

One of Bounderby's characteristic boasts is that he uses language to state simply what is the case, no more and no less. The circus community, as one would expect, does not use language in this way. Compare the description of Bounderby's front door with the description of the Pegasus Arms in Book 1, Chapter 6. The very name of Pegasus, a mythical winged horse, is a challenge to Gradgrind's rationality, and the

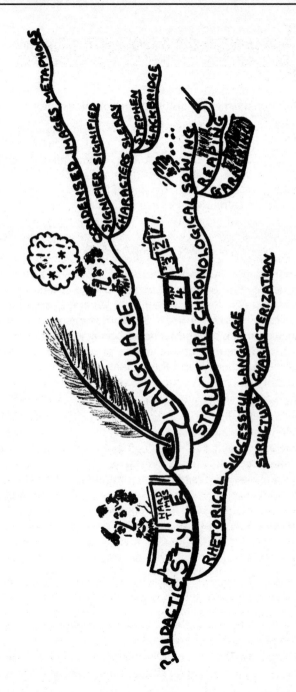

description of the pub sign is very different in style to the precise descriptions of Coketown or the houses of Bounderby and Gradgrind. When these two men encounter the circus folk in the same chapter they experience a linguistic difficulty in understanding circus slang. Sleary's manner of speaking emphasizes the alternative nature of circus society.

Dickens registers Stephen Blackpool's proletarian identity by having him speak with a working-class, northern-English accent. This is not easy to follow (at least for southerners) and perhaps this is why Dickens does not employ the same method to record the language of Rachel, even though she would be using the same regional accent. By emphasizing Stephen's working-class identity through language, however, Dickens is able to register his difference from Bounderby in the scenes where they converse together.

Interestingly, Slackbridge does not speak with a northern accent even though he is supposed to represent the interests of northern working-class people. ✪ What do you think Dickens might be suggesting about Slackbridge by not having him speak the language of those he claims to represent?

Style

There is no doubting the intention of Dickens in this novel to present a criticism of his society and his style has been described as **rhetorical** (expressed with a view to persuade). The word 'rhetorical' often carries the implication that there is something exaggerated, even false, about the manner of persuasion and this negative association is consciously evoked by some critics who use the term to describe the author's style in *Hard Times* (see 'Critical approaches', below). In the course of reading and thinking about the novel, you have to develop your opinion on this matter. If you think that the author 'lectures' the reader, merely telling you what to think and feel, then the style is **didactic**. Didacticism is a weakness in a work of literature because the reader is not being allowed to engage freely with the text as a work of imaginative fiction.

On the other hand, there is also the possibility that *Hard Times* is rhetorical in a more positive, non-didactic manner. There is nothing wrong, in principle, with a work of fiction that aims to criticize society and convince readers that its point of view is valid and valuable. If the novel is seen to succeed in terms of its language, characterization and structure, then the rhetorical and polemical (argumentative) style can be judged as successful.

You may conclude that in some, or most, parts of the novel the rhetorical style is powerfully effective whereas in some places it fails or does not succeed quite so well (see David Lodge's criticism in 'Critical approaches').

Structure

The structure of *Hard Times* follows a chronological sequence that is easy to follow. The structure is also shaped around a threefold division into Books – Sowing, Reaping and Garnering – based upon the agricultural cycle of scattering seeds (Sowing), harvesting the crop (Reaping) and then storing it (Garnering). This takes on a metaphorical significance that adds to the meaning of the novel as a whole. This division into Books was not made apparent when the story first appeared as a serial in *Household Words*. It only appeared when the novel was published as a complete book.

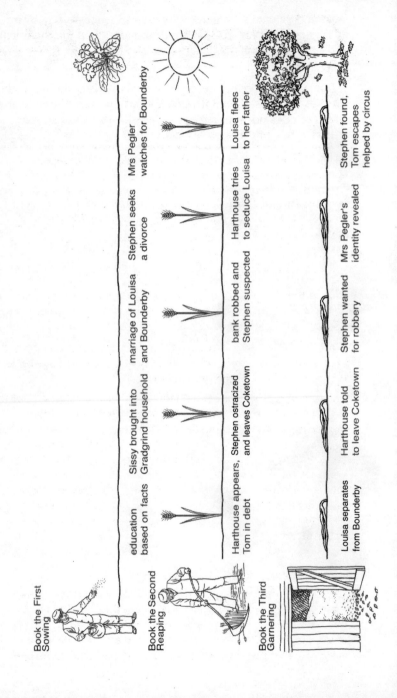

Book the First
Sowing

education
based on facts

Sissy brought into
Gradgrind household

marriage of Louisa
and Bounderby

Stephen seeks
a divorce

Mrs Pegler
watches for Bounderby

Book the Second
Reaping

Harthouse appears,
Tom in debt

Stephen ostracized
and leaves Coketown

bank robbed and
Stephen suspected

Harthouse tries
to seduce Louisa

Louisa flees
to her father

Book the Third
Garnering

Louisa separates
from Bounderby

Harthouse told
to leave Coketown

Stephen wanted
for robbery

Mrs Pegler's
identity revealed

Stephen found,
Tom escapes
helped by circus

Book the First: Sowing

Ch. 1 *The One Thing Needful*

- ◆ The novel's division into a set of books is announced.
- ◆ Gradgrind announces the importance of Facts to a class of pupils.
- ◆ Dickens' polemical style is announced.

Rι· The opening chapter is very much about announcements. The opening words are asserted by Gradgrind; they do not form a dialogue, for his listeners are not expected to reply but simply to absorb the information. He uses the verb *plant* to explain how factual information is to be transmitted in the educational process and *root out* to convey the negative process of removing unwanted ideas. People are merely *reasoning animals* and there is no place for imagination or creativity. The opening paragraph introduces what will be a central theme of the novel: the conflicting claims of reason as opposed to those of the imagination.

The terms 'reason' and 'imagination', as they are fleshed out in the course of the story, will come to represent a complex opposition of forces. Indeed the two words will become verbal shorthand for a rich and varied theme. But in this opening chapter the theme is introduced in a classroom situation, in an educational **context**. The last paragraph pictures Gradgrind's view of education as a very rational process whereby the mind of the learner is like an empty vessel which simply needs filling up with facts. ✪ How far has your own education treated you in this way?

✎ STRUCTURE AND LANGUAGE

The use of farming imagery from the Bible would have been readily picked up by Dickens' readers in the title Sowing for the first of the three books that structure *Hard Times*. The type of seed planted in the process of sowing and the place where it is sown will determine what can later be gathered or reaped, and 'as ye sow, so shall ye reap' is a quotation from the New Testament suggesting that our present behaviour will affect future events in our life. The significance of this will become apparent as the novel unfolds to show how Gradgrind's theory of education affects children, especially his own. The fact that Gradgrind himself uses words like *plant* and *root out* reminds the reader again of this biblical image.

There is another biblical reference in the title of the first chapter (Luke x, 42). ✪ Look up this reference to see what relevance it has to this chapter.

✐ STYLE AND LANGUAGE

Dickens likes to repeat a word, phrase or idea in order to emphasize something important and in this chapter he describes five aspects of Gradgrind's appearance as *square*. ✪ When someone is described as a square (it is still sometimes used as a slang expression), what is suggested? Dickens makes the educational theory that Gradgrind promotes seem inadequate by the way in which he describes the speaker.

In one sense, Dickens' own style of writing is the very opposite of Gradgrind's philosophy because it is so colourful. The simple fact that Gradgrind has a bald patch is rendered in a highly imaginative and comic manner that involves an image of fir trees and a plum pie. The overall effect is an incredible exaggeration that makes Gradgrind seem both ridiculous and unpleasant.

Dickens' style is particularly polemical in this chapter, as if imitating the doctrinaire style of Gradgrind, but the rhetoric is effectively handled and controlled through the repetition of words like *fact* (which appears ten times) and *emphasis*. Geometrical and linear terms like *square*, *line* and *inclined plane* suggest a barren and inflexible state of mind that morphs Gradgrind the individual with his narrow philosophy of life. ✪ Underline all the words in the first chapter that contribute to this sense of a one-dimensional world.

Ch. 2 *Murdering the Innocents*   *R℮*

◆ Gradgrind's philosophy is further described.
◆ Description of Bitzer who goes on to define a horse.

♦ School inspector condemns imagination.
♦ Mr M'Choakumchild takes over the class.

Rₑ· The opening paragraph represents, as we are told in the second paragraph, the way Gradgrind *always mentally introduced himself*; in other words, this is the way he thinks of himself, with the *always* suggesting that perhaps he has a need to reassure himself on this score. His self-image is alarmingly narrow and unimaginative, for he inhabits a mental world where everything is cut and dried, quantifiable, and absolute. He will not allow the complexities of people's personalities to bother him because he can quantify *any parcel of human nature* and subject anything to his notion of reason. Behind the characteristic exaggeration of Dickens' style we sense a man who insists to himself that life is straightforward, and who will not allow anyone to convince him otherwise.

Bitzer's excessively unimaginative definition of a horse is followed by the school inspector's laughable demonstration of how to go about choosing wallpaper and carpet based upon empirical principles. Behind the **parody** lies Dickens' indignation at the poverty of an education system that reduces its curriculum to the practical and the quantifiable at the expense of imagination and creativity. The seriousness of this criticism will become clearer as the story unfolds and we see the kind of adult that Bitzer, a willing subscriber to this rigidly narrow education, becomes. In contrast to this will be the kind of adult that Sissy becomes by resisting this philosophy. ❸ If you have read the whole novel, what kind of a person does Bitzer grow up to become?

✒ STYLE AND LANGUAGE

The idea that Gradgrind has repressed his own capacity for imagination was hinted at in the image from Chapter 1 of a one-dimensional *square* person. His aggressive nature was also hinted at there and now it is reinforced in the violent image of a loaded weapon and the industrial image of a *galvanizing apparatus*. Together, these images evoke the forced and unnatural regime of an education system that denies any role to the imagination. This idea of violence and repression is strengthened from the outset by the chapter's title, with its biblical overtone referring to Herod's massacre of young children (Matthew ii, 16). The idea of education as an assault on the defenceless is maintained in the boxing metaphors that describe the school inspector.

Dickens brings his characters alive and creates a sense of personality by building around them a set of associations through the use of images and vivid descriptions, as in the case of Gradgrind. Another example is in the description of sunlight playing on the faces of Bitzer and Sissy in the classroom. Bitzer's poverty of spirit is contrasted with Sissy's natural vitality through the way the light brightens up the face of one while seeming to drain the other of what little natural colour is left in it.

Another aspect of Dickens' style is evident in the names that he gives to some of his characters. A name may have an **onomatopoeic** quality so that the sound of the word evokes meaningful associations, or the name may evoke a particular image with a suggestive meaning. The two syllables of 'Grad-grind' have a harsh and unforgiving sound and the word 'grind' suggests tedium. ✪ What does 'M'Choakumchild' suggest? Note, too, that Bitzer is never called by his first name and the reader never finds out what it is. ✪ Can you suggest a suitable first name for him?

Ch. 3 *A Loophole* $R\dot{\ell}$

◆ Gradgrind walking home to Stone Lodge.
◆ Louisa and Tom are spotted peeping into the circus.
◆ Gradgrind reprimands them and Bounderby is mentioned.

This chapter brings to an end the first instalment of *Hard Times* that appeared on 1 April 1854. By the end of the instalment two quite different families have emerged: readers know more about the *eminently practical* Gradgrind and his two children than about Sissy Jupe and her father, but an important contrast has been established.

$R\dot{\ell}$ The description of Gradgrind's house, Stone Lodge, emphasizes its symmetry and straight lines, and its unexciting functionality is seen to complement the dull reasonableness of its owner. It comes as no surprise to learn that his children are unacquainted with the irrational magic of fairytales and nonsense rhymes. Louisa and Tom have been encouraged instead to collect and classify objects and arrange them in neat cabinets. It has not completely destroyed their curiosity and they are drawn to the circus because it represents what their schooling lacks.

The description of the circus is full of colour and activity: a band playing noisy music, a flag flying, a dog performing, Sissy's father defying the logic of science in his stage act and then dressing up as a fictional character. The contrast with the drab Stone Lodge is deliberate and clear-cut and we are left in no doubt that the circus, appealing to the imagination, represents an alternative to the ordered reason of Gradgrind's world.

The first two chapters have had an educational context for the presentation of the reason and imagination theme but in this chapter we begin to see the same idea being explored within a family context. Gradgrind is pleased with the way he has brought up his children and we are told he is *an affectionate father, after his manner*, and cannot understand why Louisa and Tom are attracted to the circus. Tom is not willing to resist his father's authority but Louisa, who at 15 or 16 is the older, reveals a more complex character. Her imagination is said to be *starved* but she speaks of being tired but *I don't know of what – of everything, I think.*

Gradgrind is a well-meaning parent but his children do not seem to be very happy, and this brings together the theme of parents with that of imagination and reason. Gradgrind's philosophy of education will be put to the test because the reader will watch Tom and Louisa growing up under a system of thought that places no value on imagination.

STRUCTURE

The first three chapters were read as one instalment and there was a week to wait for the next instalment. Characters have been introduced and, although nothing startling has happened yet, many readers would have picked up on the mention of Bounderby at the very end, not least because of Louisa's unusual reaction. She seems an interesting character and the reader is left wondering why she subjects her father to an *intense and searching* look when he mentions Bounderby.

Time to reflect

❓ Number the following characters in order, according to how far you think Dickens identifies them with reason, as opposed to imagination: Sissy Jupe, Bitzer, Gradgrind, Louisa, Tom. Note down at least one piece of evidence per character for your ordering.

❓ Answer the following, choosing from (a) school inspector, (b) Bitzer, (c) Gradgrind, (d) Tom, (e) the pupils (Answers on p. 87):

1 Who is going to be filled to the brim with facts?

2 Who is threatened by his own neckcloth?

3 Whose blood might be white and not red?

4 Who is willing to be taken home like a machine?

5 Who could knock the wind out of common sense?

Now take a break – do something that the Gradgrind children would be denied!

Ch. 4 *Mr Bounderby* *Re*

◆ Bounderby tells of his deprived childhood.
◆ Bounderby calls for Sissy's expulsion from school.
◆ Louisa tries to rub away any mark of Bounderby's kiss.

Bounderby presents himself as a self-made man, *with nobody to thank for my being here, but myself*, who has made a success of himself in spite of inadequate parenting. He accuses his mother of having deserted him, *bolted*, and his grandmother of being a selfish alcoholic whom he had the good fortune to run away from as soon as he was able. This portrait of grossly inadequate parents, which turns out to be a complete fiction, contrasts with the Gradgrind children's very real parents, who are inadequate in a less dramatic manner.

Look again at the study scene that Gradgrind looks in on at the end of the chapter: Louisa sadly bored, Thomas quietly crying and the young Jane *fallen asleep over vulgar fractions*. Two other children, named after noted economists of the age, are said to be away at a lecture, *in custody* – as if they are prisoners.

Bounderby himself plays the part of a kindly parent figure and kisses the reluctant Louisa before he leaves. ✪ Why do you think Louisa objects so strongly to Bounderby kissing her? Note that Tom is a witness to this and he can be in no doubt about his sister's feelings for Bounderby.

Re Mrs Gradgrind is presented as a victim of the complete defeat of the imagination at the expense of a hollow notion of reason. Any vestige of imagination she might once have possessed has been vigorously suppressed for *whenever she showed a symptom of coming to life,* [she] *was invariably stunned by some weighty piece of fact tumbling on her.* Her lack of imagination accounts for her lack of a personality and because *nobody minded her* she hardly registers as a person with her family and acquaintances. As if to confirm her insignificance, she appears in only five of the book's chapters.

In the paragraph beginning *In truth*, where Mrs Gradgrind reprimands her children for peeping at the circus, we learn that her lack of imagination is one of the reasons why Gradgrind married her. In this sense she brings her lack of a personality into her marriage, but she should also be seen as a married woman who is never known by any name but *Mrs Gradgrind* and who only seems to function within the domestic context.

She is comically ineffective as a parent – *Go and be something-ological directly*, but more sadly she has never been recognized as a person by her husband. This is hinted at in the description of her as a *transparency of a small female figure, without enough light behind it.* She lacks her own light; nor does anyone else give her enough love or attention to make up for it.

In the paragraph that follows the *In truth* one above, we are told that just being in the company of her husband and Bounderby is *sufficient to stun* her into social invisibility. Her inadequacy is all the more obvious in the company of two men whose poverty of imagination and complacency leave no space for a woman like her.

STYLE AND LANGUAGE

Here, as in Chapter 1, Dickens creates a sense of character not by psychological analysis, but by imaginatively exaggerating physical appearance. With Bounderby, a host of details are alluded to that work together to bring this most unpleasant individual to life. We are told about his *stare*, how he laughs, his *puffed* head and *swelled veins* and his skin so *strained* that he resembles a balloon.

Dickens works through parody and caricature, and because the immediate effect is a humorous one it is easy to downplay this aspect of his style and miss the serious point that he is making. Bounderby is a fraud, full of false platitudes about his childhood, as insubstantial as the air inside a balloon. Perhaps this is what Dickens is suggesting through words like *puffed* and *swelled*.

The author also points to Bounderby's lack of hair, a feature he shares with Gradgrind (Chapter 1), and this is taken too as an indication of his character. The few disordered hairs, we are told, are like this because of being *constantly blown about by his windy boastfulness*. ✪ Look at some cartoons of famous people to see how caricature can be used to comment on character.

Ch. 5 *The Key-Note* $R\ell^{\cdot}$

◆ Coketown introduced and described.
◆ Sissy is chased by Bitzer.
◆ Gradgrind and Bounderby are brought to Sissy's home.

Coketown is the town where a circus happens to arrive, where a school happens to be and where a certain Mr Bounderby happens to own a factory. The town though is far more than just the background for a set of events; it is also the physical and cultural expression of the industrial revolution that transformed people's lives during the nineteenth century. For Dickens, Coketown is the archetypal expression of industrial capitalism and he describes its bleakness and pollution, in both material and spiritual terms. ❂ Do you think anywhere matching this description still exists?

In the third paragraph the reader is reminded of the gulf between the dismal monotony of Coketown life and the elegance of what is produced here for the benefit of a different social class whose members *could scarcely bear to hear the place mentioned*. The long sixth paragraph develops this theme by cataloguing how various middle-class institutions and individuals – the Church, the Teetotal Society, chemist, jail chaplain, Bounderby and Gradgrind – all despair of Coketown's working-class inhabitants.

R̬ The overlap between the theme of capitalism and that of reason and imagination is marked in this chapter's opening paragraph when Coketown is declared a *triumph of fact* and a place devoid of *fancy*, Dickens' word for the imagination. The monotonous layout of streets and houses mirrors a factory life that imposes a relentless routine of dull work and destroys people's chance to enjoy their leisure. The Church's failure to help is suggested by a church built in the same unimaginative architectural style as the factories: a *pious warehouse of red brick*. Dickens implies that it cannot offer any spiritual alternative either.

The overlap is made explicit in the paragraph that begins with the rhetorical question *Is it possible, I wonder, that there was any analogy between the case of the Coketown population and the case of the little Gradgrinds?* The community's need for recreation is mirrored by the individual's need to exercise the imagination. Gradgrind's children, pictured at the end of Chapter 4 as sad and unfulfilled, are a microcosm of the deprivation of Coketown life as a whole. Notice that this idea cuts across social class and unites the well-off Gradgrinds with the anonymous working poor of Coketown.

❂ Where are we told that Gradgrind is not as heartless a parent as we might fear? Bounderby, the bully of children as well as of humility, scares young Sissy Jupe and it may be this that causes Gradgrind to try and reassure her. We are told that his parental character was formed by *arithmetic* and that he would have been a kinder parent if the arithmetic had not balanced. Words like *arithmetic* and *fact* are used by Dickens as binary opposites of imagination and they come to represent the kind of heartless reason that is responsible for so many social and family ills. Here we see the theme of parents overlapping with that of reason and imagination.

✒ STYLE AND LANGUAGE

The second paragraph brings Coketown to life through two startling images. The comparison of industrial smoke emanating from the factories like coiled serpents that *trailed themselves for ever and ever* suggests something infinite and satanic while a factory engine which is compared to the nodding head of a deranged elephant is seen as part of the organized insanity that characterizes life in Coketown.

In the paragraph mentioned above, beginning *Is it possible, I wonder, that there was any analogy ...,* we see Dickens' **polemical** (argumentative) style. He directly addresses the reader, who is asked to consider whether imaginative play is not as important to adults as it is to children. A criticism of Dickens here is that he does not allow this question to emerge from the writing, as it does elsewhere. One could argue that being polemical is a part of Dickens' style and has to be accepted as such. It is not that he is forcing his opinion on the reader, but simply that he likes to state it. ✪ What do you think about this?

✒ STRUCTURE

This chapter's title, *The Key-Note,* announces the importance of Coketown in Dickens' story. From the point of view of plot and structure the town is at the heart of *Hard Times* because this is where the story unfolds and Coketown is known to all the characters in the novel. The fact that the story centres on one town underlines the tight structure of a plot that brings together a relatively small number of characters whose paths criss-cross in the course of events.

Although there is a subplot to *Hard Times,* the novel is remarkably streamlined for Dickens. Some of his novels are complicated by the large number of characters and by multi-layered plots. By comparison, the structure of *Hard Times* is straightforward and all the characters are involved, one way or another, with Coketown. As well as being at the centre of the plot, Coketown is at the philosophical heart of the novel.

Ch. 6 *Sleary's Horsemanship* $R\acute{c}$

◆ Sissy is unable to find her father.
◆ Childers explains her father's disappearance.
◆ Sissy leaves the circus to begin a new life with the Gradgrinds.

$R\acute{c}$ Look again at the fifth paragraph, that describes Gradgrind and Bounderby standing alone in Jupe's room. The two men, ambassadors for a world of reason and facts, stand and wait in a room distinguished by a night-cap embellished by two peacock feathers and rendered comic by a pigtail that stands upright in it. The object can be seen as an image for the play of the imagination, for what night-cap would have feathers and how could a pigtail remain vertical? The night-cap itself is not a recurrent image but the circus generally comes to represent the life of the imagination – an alternative to the world of facts. Sissy has to choose whether to remain in the circus or leave it for the world of Gradgrind and Bounderby.

Reason and imagination are not treated simplistically by Dickens. The terms are not polar opposites, like black and white, because we see circus people like Childers and Sleary exhibiting a clear sense of reason and a grasp of the importance of facts. Indeed, when Bounderby's rudeness finally exasperates the patient Childers the hard-headed businessman is reprimanded with the words: *I am telling your friend what's the fact; if you don't like it, you can avail yourself of the open air.* The difference is that the circus people do not worship reason and facts at the expense of all else. ✪ Can you find a line spoken by Sleary, near the end of this chapter, that expresses this point?

The circus people's natural goodness comes to the fore in their response to the plight Sissy finds herself in after her father's disappearance. Their sympathy for Sissy is heartfelt and Sleary speaks for all of them when he offers her a loving home with them. Dickens spells out their qualities: *a special inaptitude for any kind of sharp practice, and an untiring readiness to help and pity one another.* This might seem a little sentimental but there is also the fact that they are likely to manhandle Bounderby out of the house for his insensitivity towards Sissy. Nor does Kidderminster mince his words when dealing with Bounderby.

Sissy Jupe's father has deserted her but Childers explains that he has acted out of love. Jupe cannot bear to see his daughter hurt and embarrassed by him being *goosed* (hissed by a disappointed audience), so he has left her to pursue her education without the encumbrance of a failing father to look after. It seems that this act of generosity has moved Gradgrind because he offers to fulfil her father's wishes by giving her a home with his family. ✪ How do we know that Bounderby tries to change Gradgrind's mind about adopting Sissy?

STRUCTURE

Chapters 4 and 5 made up the second instalment in the serialization of *Hard Times*, and this chapter, the longest in the first Book of the novel, provided an instalment in itself. This underlines its structural importance. By the end of the chapter the central theme of reason and imagination has been dramatized through the world of Gradgrind and Bounderby and the alternative world of the circus. Sissy's decision is the culminating point of this chapter and it brings the two worlds together by bringing a child of the circus into Gradgrind's life.

STYLE AND LANGUAGE

In Sleary's speech Dickens attempts to capture in writing his pronunciation problem over sibilant 's' sounds by reducing them in writing to *th*. ✪ How effective is this? How does it affect your reading?

It takes an effort to comprehend Sleary but Dickens chose to render his speech in this way in order to emphasize his difference from the world of Bounderby and Gradgrind. Sleary and the circus are not of their world; they represent an alternative set of values and Dickens tries to represent this in language. In the same way, there is a profusion of slang expressions, like *goosed, stow that* ('stop what you're doing') and *pay your ochre* (show your money), associated with the circus people. Their difference is emphasized by the fact that people like Gradgrind cannot, literally, understand what they are saying. At a philosophical level, nor can they understand the values that the circus represents.

Now try these exercises

? Find a quote from Chapters 4–6 to support each of these statements. See if your teacher agrees with you.

Bounderby is 47 or 48 years old.

Bounderby suggests that Sissy be asked to leave the school.

Gradgrind and Bounderby do not know their way about working-class districts of Coketown.

Bounderby thinks Sissy has been out getting gin for her father.

It was Jupe's idea to send his daughter to school in Coketown.

? Try this quiz (Answers on p. 87):

(a) Who is *the Bully of humility*?

(b) Whose head is in a state of *melancholy madness*?

(c) Who looks at whom with *mingled astonishment and dread*?

(d) Who drove a Greek chariot through towns?

? Reread the second paragraph of Chapter 5. Then draw a picture of Coketown. Include: brick buildings, machinery, smoke, tall chimneys, a canal, a river, and residential streets.

So many facts! Have a rest

Ch. 7 *Mrs Sparsit*   R¿

◆ Bounderby converses with his housekeeper, Mrs Sparsit.
◆ Gradgrind turns up to collect Sissy Jupe.

This chapter introduces Mrs Sparsit and her relationship with Bounderby. Dickens summarizes Mrs Sparsit's family connection with Lady Scadgers, and, through her deceased husband, with the Powlers. In so doing, he does not disguise his contempt for the idle rich. Bounderby relishes having Mrs Sparsit as his housekeeper because he sees it as a way of highlighting his own social success. ❻ How do we know that Mrs Sparsit enjoys her own sense of a superior social background?

 Mrs Sparsit has none of the virtues attributed to the circus people at the end of the last chapter. Dickens does not explicitly state here that she is insincere, cunning, and jealously aware of Bounderby's interest in Louisa but he describes her in a way that makes the reader feel very uneasy about her. The closing sentence of the chapter hints strongly at her secretive nature, in contrast with the open and frank nature of Sleary and the circus people.

STYLE AND LANGUAGE

Dickens suggests character through physical appearance and mannerisms. Mrs Sparsit's distinguishing traits are her high-bridged nose and dense black eyebrows. When Louisa's name first crops up in her conversation with Bounderby, we see in Mrs Sparsit *a slight expansion of the nostrils* and a contraction of *her black eyebrows*. The unpleasant image, vaguely reptilian, leaves the reader feeling suspicious of her motives.

Ch. 8 *Never Wonder* R^i

♦ Gradgrind disapproves of *wonder*.
♦ Louisa gazes into a fire and talks with Tom.

R^i Although beginning and ending with an admonishment to 'never wonder', the impulse to do just that is what emerges most strongly from the chapter. Gradgrind is perplexed to know that works of fiction, mere *fancy*, are popular in the local library. His son Tom feels imprisoned while his daughter Louisa finds release in letting her imagination wander as she gazes at the sparks of a fire.

The sad results of Gradgrind's philosophy are seen in the gloomy scene where Tom and Louisa's conversation reveals the inadequacies of their upbringing. Tom almost feels sorry for Sissy Jupe being subjected to the same educational regime. His name for the *parental roof* is a *Jaundiced Jail*, and Gradgrind the parent thus becomes the jailer. It is Louisa who provides Tom with affection, and even at this age he sees how he can use her, recognizing Bounderby's designs on his *little pet.*

The parents theme overlaps with the reason and imagination theme when Gradgrind's failure as a parent is realized in terms of the poverty of his educational system and its effect on these two children. A strict adherence to facts and the denial of imagination can lead to a breakdown in rationality itself, and the chapter ends with the wittering nonsense of their mother.

✍ STYLE AND LANGUAGE

A good example of Dickens' skill in condensing the pace of change and creating a language that works in a highly imaginative manner is the description of the shadow on the wall of their room. It follows on immediately from Tom's talk of knowing how to *smoothe old Bounderby,* and the shadow cast on the wall by the cupboards (the *presses*) evokes the image of Bounderby as a brooding and intrusive presence on their young lives. Dickens creates and maintains a personality in his characters by elliptical sketches, often featuring their appearance or mannerisms, or descriptive images like this one of Bounderby.

Ch. 9 *Sissy's Progress* *Ré*

◆ Sissy talks to Louisa about life at school.
◆ Sissy talks to Louisa about her father.

Sissy's answer to the question of what is the first principle of political economy, a subject that we would now just call economics, is both funny and subversive. Her *absurd* answer, given at the end of the third paragraph, posits an alternative to capitalism by suggesting a principle of mutual aid instead of self-interest.

When Sissy is asked a question about prosperity her reply is that the nature of prosperity depends on how wealth is distributed and not the quantifiable total value of that prosperity. ❂ Can you find the words spoken by Sissy that make this point?

Ré Sissy, as a child of the circus, has an alternative view of the world to the world propounded by the educational system in which she finds herself. Her isolation within this system but also the validity of her way of understanding and judging the world, is brought out in her response to her teacher's questions. She does not deny facts she is presented with but she steadfastly questions the conventional and national interpretation of them – 25 is a very tiny percentage of 1,000,000 – by insisting on bringing an emotional and imaginative perspective into the equation. Thus she insists on thinking about, imagining, the human aspect of the plight of statistically insignificant numbers of individuals.

❂ What percentage of 1,000,000 is 25? Why is it different to speak of 0.0025% starving to death as opposed to saying 25 people suffered this fate? ❂ What percentage of 100,000 is 500? Do you agree with Sissy that, looked at from one point of view, the answer to the last question doesn't mean anything?

It is only Sissy's attachment to her father that has prevented her from running away from her new home with Gradgrind. This confirms Tom's opinion in the chapter before that *they'll bother her head off,* his way of describing the relentless tedium of an education under Gradgrind's philosophy. The strength of a loving bond between parent and child is borne out by Sissy's determination to stay, just as the dismay experienced by Tom and Louisa is testimony to the failure of a parent–child bond based purely on rational calculation.

Gradgrind, for all his faults, is not immune to emotion and it is ironic that he can be filled with pity at the realization that Sissy is not happy and yet fail to detect another kind of unhappiness in his own children. Louisa asks Sissy questions about her parents as if she wants confirmation that an alternative family life to her own could actually exist: *were you his comfort?, your father was always kind? and to make people laugh?*

Louisa is keen to question Sissy about the relationship between her father and mother – *Did your father love her?* – and the strength of the impulse behind Louisa's curiosity is made clear by Dickens who describes how she *asked these questions with a strong, wild, wandering interest peculiar to her; an interest gone astray like a banished creature, and hiding in solitary places.* The meaning behind this image is not transparently clear but for a clue look at the last paragraph of this chapter, which suggests there is not much of a loving relationship between Mr and Mrs Gradgrind. ✪ What do you think Dickens is suggesting by describing Louisa's curiosity in the way that he does?

Ch. 10 *Stephen Blackpool* R²

◆ Stephen waits for Rachel at the end of a working day.
◆ Stephen and Rachel walk home and talk together.
◆ Stephen finds his estranged wife asleep in his room.

Coketown is described as an unnatural conurbation, brought into existence as a place of work and where people are huddled together *for some one man's purpose*, the *one man* referring to the entrepreneur who happens to own a particular factory. The town as a whole has already been described (Chapter 5) and in this chapter the area where the working class live is brought into focus. ✪ How does the description of Coketown in the second paragraph of Chapter 5 compare with that in the second paragraph of this chapter?

Dickens describes the working class as a *race*, emphasizing their fixed and separate identity. The social gulf between them and their employers is brought out in the startling image of a primeval life-form from the sea that only has some means of motion and a stomach to fuel itself. This, we are informed, is how *some people* (i.e. the employers) would have preferred nature to provide them with the means of running and working their factories.

The problem of Stephen's marriage is first alluded to by Rachel when she remarks *Let the laws be,* referring to the law that keeps Stephen married to someone he would like to divorce but cannot. The first readers of *Hard Times* could only guess that this might be the law referred to; the identity of the strange woman in his room would remain a mystery at this stage. This instalment comes to an exciting conclusion and readers had a week to wait before finding out about Stephen's wife and marriage.

LANGUAGE AND STYLE

Dickens differentiated the circus people by their manner of speaking and he does something similar with working-class people. The speech of Stephen Blackpool is distinguished by an attempt to capture the northern working-class accent, so that 'I thought you were behind me' is rendered *I thought thou wast ahind me* and 'it might make people talk, even of you' becomes *t' might mak fok talk, even of thee.* ✪ Why do you think Dickens goes to the trouble of trying to render speech-patterns in this way?

Notice how for Dickens the physical pollution of Coketown mirrors a sense of social defilement in the way people are forced to live together in squalid conditions. This comes out in the image of the contorted shapes of chimneys, signalling the poor quality of life awaiting the buildings' occupants. Death is a constant in this ghetto life, evoked by the presence of the undertaker's ladder ready to receive a coffin from a window above.

Organizing some thoughts

❓ Fill in the missing word in the following quotations and ask yourself what the quote reveals about a character or a theme in the novel. Learn the quotations by heart; they can be used later in an essay.

[Mrs Sparsit's nose] *underwent a slight expansion of the nostrils, and her black … contracted as she took a sip of tea.*

under the influence of that … piece of fact, she would become torpid again.

The shadow of their subject, and of its lowering association with their …

❓ Dickens builds up two contrasting and conflicting worlds, that of Coketown and that of the circus, by associating each of them with particular words and images. Sort out the quotations below by using a coloured pen to mark those that belong to the circus. What differences between the two worlds is Dickens intent on drawing out?

stutterings (Ch. 9)

all the fathers could dance upon rolling casks, stand upon bottles, catch knives and balls (Ch. 6)

Make the betht of uth; not the wurtht (Ch. 6)

narrow courts upon courts, and close streets upon streets (Ch. 10)

looked a most remarkable sort of Centaur (Ch. 6)

a town of unnatural red and black (Ch. 5)

white nightcap, embellished with two peacock's feathers and a pigtail bolt upright

? Name the character referred to:

he died of alcoholism aged 24

he slept on paving stones

she slept on feathered pillows

he looked older than he was

she is 35, has black hair and an oval face

? At this stage in the book a number of important relationships have been introduced. Draw lines from each of the words below to the relationship which you think is best described by the word. Some lines might come from the same word more than once:

> Mr and Mrs Gradgrind
>
> Sissy's father and mother
>
> Mrs Sparsit and Bounderby
>
> Bounderby and Louisa
>
> Louisa and Tom
>
> Stephen Blackpool and Rachel

calculating   cold   affectionate   passionless
self-interested   tender   scheming.

? Think of a word or phrase to describe the nature of each relationship above.

Ch. 11 *No Way Out*

◆ Stephen at work bent over his loom.

♦ Stephen's lunchtime visit to Bounderby for advice about divorce.

♦ Stephen is told there is nothing he can do about his marriage.

The opening few paragraphs draw a dismal picture of industrial capitalism and the worker reduced to being an ancillary piece of equipment, a part of the relentless machinery that momentarily pauses only for lunchtime. Dickens ponders what it would be like if a system could run *by other means.* ○ What do you think he is suggesting?

The class difference between workers like Stephen and employers like Bounderby is expressed through food. Stephen has only some bread for his lunch while Bounderby tucks into a meat chop with sherry. The employer's first suspicion is that his visitor might be asking about improved wages or conditions at work, looking in other words for *turtle soup and venison.* His suspicions are later confirmed when Stephen has the temerity to call the law about divorce *a muddle* and by implication suggest that social class should not determine access to the law.

When Mrs Sparsit offers to leave them alone, Bounderby reacts with a pompous declaration of her social importance. The vulgarity of the importance he attaches to social class is brought out in the description of how he waves her back from her pretence of leaving while his other hand momentarily grasps his chop. He then swallows a mouthful of meat and proceeds to lecture Stephen on his social inferiority before someone like Mrs Sparsit. The unpleasant picture this draws of Bounderby at his dinner table mirrors the ugliness of his ideas about class.

The misery of Stephen's unfortunate marriage is spelt out for Bounderby and the reader and there is nothing sentimental in the telling of the consequences of a broken marriage. Bounderby's blunt observation that Stephen is powerless to act reduces him to the insignificance which also characterizes his value as an individual worker.

Mrs Sparsit makes her own snide contributions by pretending to ask innocently whether there was a marked difference of age between Stephen and his wife. Bounderby has good reason to look askance at her with a look of *odd sheepishness.* She is clearly thinking about the age-gap between Bounderby and young Louisa, and her barbed question is intended to cause discomfort. Mrs Sparsit's own marriage, now very much broken, did involve a significant age difference. ✪ How closely do you read the text? Do you remember how much older Mrs Sparsit is than her husband? Look back to Chapter 7 if necessary.

LANGUAGE AND STYLE

An example of Dickens' condensed style in drawing and animating a broad canvas of society while keeping within the strict writing demands of weekly instalments is to be seen in the opening paragraphs. Each of the first two sentences refers back to earlier descriptions: the *Fairy palaces* being first mentioned in the fifth paragraph of Chapter 10, and the *melancholy mad elephants* echoing the opening description of Coketown in Chapter 5. Pictured within this industrial metropolis is the self-absorbed Stephen, a typical worker who emerges from *the forest of looms* as a human being, one of the anonymous *hands*, amidst a cacophony of machines and motion.

Immediately following this cameo portrait, in the third paragraph, is a philosophical reflection on the immense difficulty of understanding human nature and the mystery of people as compared to the predictability of a machine.

Ch. 12 *The Old Woman* $R\ell$

◆ Stephen is questioned by Bounderby's mother.
◆ Stephen reflects on his doomed marriage.

The reader is left to guess the identity of the strange woman who accosts Stephen as he is leaving for work. Knowing that she is Bounderby's mother, however, makes sense of her behaviour and attitude. As a parent she is filled with pride and admiration for the kind of man she thinks her son has become. The irony of this is particularly piquant given that we have just witnessed the encounter between Stephen and her son and the reader has a very good idea of the kind of person he has grown into. Like the other parent–child relationships in the novel, this one does not betoken a happy state of affairs.

Bounderby's mother, however, is blissfully happy – because of her ignorance; Stephen, ironically, is painfully unhappy because of his state of knowledge. The poignancy of his situation presses in on him as he imagines the kind of life he could be living with Rachel. ❷ Given that Stephen's kind of marital problem is not so likely to occur in modern Britain or the US, do you think the emotional impact of Stephen's plight is weakened for a modern audience?

A clear moral distinction is made between characters like Bounderby and Mrs Sparsit and other characters like Sissy, Rachel or Stephen. The depth of insincerity of some of the characters is what the novel unfolds in the course of its tale while in this chapter there are telling little reminders of what makes Stephen and Bounderby's mother quite different. Stephen leaves the house and, prompted by the mark his hot hand had left on the polished metal, wipes it clean without thinking. Stephen does this for its own sake. He is not being slavish, because he has a natural sincerity that reveals itself in such ordinary ways.

Although some readers find Stephen a difficult character to believe in, he is portrayed as someone who is too sincere for his own good. He is almost saintly in his role as the patient, suffering victim who tortures himself with thoughts of how happy he and Rachel could be. ❷ Do you think he is just too virtuous to engage the reader's interest? Can you empathize with a character even if you are not especially interested in the kind of person he or she is?

Bounderby's mother is driven by the strength of her parental devotion and this reveals itself in her extraordinary annual pilgrimage to catch a glimpse of her son. Like Stephen, she is perhaps too sincere in her own beliefs. She asks Stephen if he is happy because she cannot but believe that anyone working for her son would be more than content. As with Stephen, there is a naivety about her but it is well meant.

Ch. 13 *Rachel* Rᵉ

◆ Stephen returns home to find Rachel caring for his sick wife.
◆ Stephen sleeps and is afflicted with a nightmare.
◆ Rachel prevents Stephen's wife from poisoning herself.

Dickens has been criticized for presenting his good characters, especially when they are female, as unrealistically virtuous and simply too good to believe in as three-dimensional people. Such a criticism can be directed against Rachel on the grounds that her sincerity and depth of charity are exaggerated. ✪ Do you find Rachel a difficult person to believe in? Try to give an example from this chapter to support your opinion.

The effect of Stephen's disastrous marriage on his physical well-being was brought out in the fourth paragraph of Chapter 10. ✪ Can you recall any of the details used there to describe his physical appearance? This chapter reveals the damage to his mental state, first touched on when he notices the bottle of poison. He tells Rachel that this gave him a *fright*: he realizes that the death of his wife would solve his problems. His nightmare carries this thought further as his subconscious torments him with the idea of his execution, which follows, presumably, from his complicity in the death of his wife.

LANGUAGE AND STYLE

Dickens liked to use images of natural light to describe character and suggest personality. ✪ Can you remember how Sissy and Bitzer were first introduced in Chapter 2? In the fourth paragraph of this chapter we are told how *the light of her* [Rachel's] *face shone in upon the midnight of his mind.* The full force of this metaphor is then brought home by the revelation of Stephen's tormented thoughts about the desirability of his wife's death, because it is not only Rachel's physical presence that prevents the woman from killing herself but the influence of her presence in his life that gives him the moral strength to go on living with some dignity.

Imagery of light brings the chapter to a close by comparing Rachel's uplifting effect on his depression to that of the force of starlight as against that of a candle.

This chapter is tremendously theatrical. A storm rages outside the house where Rachel cares for Stephen's wife, while inside the quiet bedroom Stephen's mind undergoes its own stormy passage as he finds himself wishing his wife was dead and then drawing back in horror at his own inhumanity and realizing that Rachel is vital to his sanity and human dignity.

The chapter ends with the clearing of the storm, mirroring the calm reconciliation within Stephen's mind.

Ch. 14 *The Great Manufacturer* Rℓ

◆ Time has passed and Louisa, Tom and Sissy are all older.
◆ Gradgrind asks to see Louisa the following morning.
◆ Tom hints at a possible marriage of Louisa and Bounderby.

Gradgrind fulfils his parental role by establishing his son Tom at work for Bounderby and, although only hints are given at this stage, it is clear that he also has plans for Louisa now that she is *quite a young woman*. Gradgrind cannot feel happy with Sissy's failure to meet the academic demands of her schooling but he shows once again that he is not heartless when he recognizes her good intentions and does not feel like judging her as a failure. ✪ Can you recall an earlier occasion when Gradgrind showed himself capable of an emotional response?

Tom is very aware of Louisa's sisterly love and he has no scruples about exploiting it in his dealings with Bounderby. Louisa's feelings, by contrast, are unblemished by any selfish considerations and this is a mark of her sincerity and goodness. This capacity to be selfless is what also comes across in Sissy's personality and it is this emotional intelligence which Gradgrind finds himself responding to in the paragraph, in the middle of the chapter, beginning *He really liked Sissy too well to have a contempt for her.*

LANGUAGE, STYLE AND STRUCTURE

The previous four chapters were devoted to the **subplot** involving Stephen Blackpool. Dickens begins this chapter by suggesting that a period of some years has now passed in the lives of the main characters. The three children have all grown up and Gradgrind himself is now an MP. We are still in Book the First, 'Sowing', but the passing of time suggests that this first phase of the story is now coming to an end.

In the middle of this chapter, in the paragraph beginning *All this while, Louisa had been passing on*, we again see Louisa gazing into a fire as she did at the end of Chapter 8. ✪ Can you recall what she was then thinking when she gazed into the fire before? The transient nature of fire and ashes becomes an image for the nature of time and in the final paragraph of this chapter Dickens uses a mixed metaphor of fire and the spinning of thread to ponder on the uncertainty and mystery of time. The style is very condensed, as indeed this whole chapter has to be in order to convey the passage of years, but Dickens manages it with great skill.

Read the last paragraph again. ✪ Can you see how Louisa, the passage of time, Coketown and its factory are all brought together in the language and images? What good reason is there for thinking that the end of this chapter concluded another week's instalment of *Hard Times* when it first appeared in 1854?

Ch. 15 *Father and Daughter* $R\ell$

◆ Gradgrind informs Louisa of Bounderby's marriage proposal.
◆ Louisa questions her father about love but accepts the proposal.
◆ Sissy and Mrs Gradgrind receive the news.

This is an important chapter and a number of themes come together and overlap.

$R\ell$ The opening paragraph describes Gradgrind as a man trapped unawares by the limitations of his own philosophy. Surrounded by the blue books of parliamentary reports, where everything is tabulated and quantified, he cannot direct his gaze upon *the teeming myriads of human beings around him*. His utilitarian and rationalistic approach prevents him from imaginatively engaging with his daughter's situation. It also creates a communication barrier that makes Louisa unable to break through and touch his heart with her predicament.

The theme of reason and imagination threads its way through the whole novel and one aspect of its unifying power is the way it accounts for Gradgrind's inadequacy as a parent in this scene with his daughter. Earlier scenes have made it clear that Gradgrind is not completely immune to emotion, but he is in the grip of a narrow philosophy that prevents him from responding to Louisa on an emotional level.

Gradgrind is not always completely in control of himself, though, and when Louisa first reacts in a very cold and controlled manner to his announcement of a marriage proposal he is a little taken aback. We are told that he is not so *collected at this moment as his daughter was* and he fidgets with a paper-knife before continuing. ✪ Why do you think he is momentarily disconcerted by Louisa's response? Her question about love discomforts him even more but instead of acknowledging its relevance he sidesteps the issue by ludicrously quoting statistics about marriage in China.

In the middle of this chapter, in the paragraph beginning *from the beginning, she had sat looking at him fixedly*, we are told why Louisa is unable to tell him what she really feels. He has no *algebra* to deal with human relations and instead he has created an *artificial barrier* that Louisa cannot surmount. There is a moment here when Louisa is on the verge of opening her heart to him but she senses that his mind is closed and the *moment shot away into the plumbless depths of the past.* ✪ If you have read the whole novel, what poignant scene towards its end does this present encounter foreshadow?

Just before their dialogue comes to an end, Louisa touches again on his inadequacy as a parent and the emotional poverty of her upbringing. She complains about never having had a *child's heart* but Gradgrind takes this as a compliment and feels assured that nothing is wrong. Behind the irony of this moment lies the unsettling picture of a parent who listens to the words of his daughter but cannot hear what she is saying.

Louisa challenges Gradgrind's utilitarian view of marriage by insistently bringing love into the equation. *Do you think I love Mr Bounderby ... do you ask me to love Mr Bounderby? ... does Mr Bounderby ask me to love him?* Gradgrind, recognizing love as something *fanciful, fantastic ... sentimental,* reasonably suggests that the term love may be *a little misplaced.* Louisa won't be sidestepped and asks for an alternative criterion by which she can make a decision. ✪ What does Gradgrind offer as an alternative? Mrs Gradgrind's observation can be interpreted as a more insightful comment on the prospects for a marriage that is not built on love. She hopes that *if your head begins to split as soon as you are married, which was the case with mine, I cannot consider that you are to be envied.*

The final paragraph registers a significant change in the relationship between Louisa and Sissy. ✪ Why do you think Louisa reacts to Sissy's look in the way that the final sentence describes? Sissy does not say anything but her look conveys *wonder ... pity ... sorrow* at the news of her impending marriage. Her recognition of some act of insincerity on Louisa's part penetrates Louisa's mind and she draws back defensively from this look of truth.

 STYLE AND LANGUAGE

The first paragraph is devoted to a **simile** (a comparison using 'as' or 'like') that helps us to understand the terrible mistake that Gradgrind makes over Louisa and the marriage proposal. The image of Gradgrind, as an astronomer within a windowless observatory who fails to check his star map against the real night sky outside the observatory, captures the sense of moral blindness with which he contemplates his daughter's future as the wife of Bounderby.

Imagery also comes to the fore in the critical moment where Gradgrind has left Louisa with the decision to make about the proposal and she sits looking silently out the window at the Coketown chimneys. When her father distracts her by asking if the chimneys can help her decide she replies enigmatically, *There seems to be nothing but languid and monotonous smoke. Yet when the night comes, Fire bursts out, father!* ✪ What do you think she means? Can you relate your reply to the reason and imagination theme?

This whole chapter demonstrates how Dickens creates meaning through imagery. He does not provide us with a systematic analysis of Louisa's state of mind, or of her father's thought processes, in the way that a more 'psychological' author might. If you are also studying Jane Austen or Shakespeare's *Hamlet*, you should imagine how these authors might have dealt with a scene like this one between Louisa and her father. ✪ Ask your teacher to suggest an example from another writer you are studying that shows a more detailed psychological analysis of character.

In place of psychological analysis Dickens gives us a rich set of images hinting at complex states of mind. In addition to the images of the astronomer and the chimney smoke, we have, in the second paragraph, a *statistical clock* that is said to beat out time like *a rap upon a coffin-lid.* ✪ What do you think Dickens is suggesting? Gradgrind is not a man given to fidgeting and yet he is described as tinkering with his paper-knife. ✪ What is being hinted at? Dickens also speaks of aspects of life which elude the *utmost cunning of algebra* and of barriers that were *too many and too high.* The reader is left to ponder these images. The chapter shows the power and effectiveness of Dickens' imagination. ✪ Read it again and underline the images that you find interesting and arresting. What are we being told about Louisa's state of mind and her father's?

Ch. 16 *Husband and Wife*   R∠

◆ Bounderby announces to Mrs Sparsit his coming marriage.
◆ The marriage takes place eight weeks later.
◆ Book the First comes to an end.

Mrs Sparsit's response to news of the marriage disconcerts Bounderby. Although it is never stated it seems likely that Mrs Sparsit would willingly have become his wife, if she had ever been asked, and that he senses this himself, hence the discomfort at the need to inform her of his engagement to Louisa. The reader may even share some of Bounderby's surprise at the calm and contented way with which she receives the news.

Everything we know about Mrs Sparsit suggests that she is not disinterestedly expressing her real feelings to Bounderby. ✪ Looking back at Chapters 7 and 9, how is it suggested that Mrs Sparsit may be a very insincere and unpleasant person? What image is again used to describe her early on in this chapter to emphasize this unpleasantness?

Bounderby is anxious to assure Mrs Sparsit that her social position will not be compromised by her moving to a room over his bank. She will continue to receive the same wage, or rather the *annual compliment* as she insists on calling it, and Bounderby is happy to employ such a euphemism notwithstanding the way he presents himself in his wedding speech as a straight-talking man who *when he see a Post, says 'that's a Post'.* In the speech he again refers to his deprived childhood as a way of exalting his present social success.

Mrs Sparsit, driven by her own selfish feelings, senses the unsoundness of Bounderby's marriage and the end of the chapter suggests that Louisa herself has some misgivings about her decision. As Tom is saying goodbye to her she gives him a hug and is *a little shaken in her reserved composure for the first time.* This comes immediately after Tom congratulates her – *what a game girl you are, to be such a first-rate sister, Loo!* – delighted as he is to have a close family connection with his employer. ✪ Why do you think Louisa feels shaken at this moment? Is there something in what Tom said that has caused her dismay?

STYLE AND LANGUAGE

The answer to the second question in the first section above, about the image used to describe Mrs Sparsit, is that of a bird of prey. As she picks out holes in a piece of cloth with a scissors, Dickens likens her to a hawk picking out the eyes of its prey. The image, hinting as it does at her callousness and vindictiveness, is another example of the author's style. Dickens, who complained in a letter to a friend that in writing this novel 'the difficulty of space is crushing', is constrained by the rigours of the weekly instalment format to keep the narrative moving within a set amount of words. There is little scope to go off at a tangent and develop minor characters, a feature that is characteristic of many of his other novels.

Given these constraints, Dickens could not afford to dwell at length on an individual character like Mrs Sparsit who is important to the plot but who is not one of the major personalities in the story. A single deft image captures her essence. ✪ Think of an image of your own that could be used to suggest her vindictive and cruel nature.

Here is a list of the chapter's important images and a mnemonic to remember them by:

> windowless astronomical observatory
> algebra that fails to read the secrets of the heart
> fidgeting with a paper-knife
> languid smoke hiding bursts of life
> clock that measures time like a rap upon a coffin-lid

When **A**lgebra **F**ails, **L**ove **C**apitulates

STRUCTURE

The novel is in three parts, and the end of the first one marks a turning-point in the story. The sowing is over and reaping is about to begin. The first Book began in spring, when Louisa and Tom were teenagers, and ends about four years later. All but one of the main characters have been introduced and so have all the important themes. These themes are closely interlocked and come together in the marriage of Louisa and Bounderby.

Against her deeper feelings Louisa, in harmony with the unemotional and strict rationalism of her father's philosophy, has married a capitalist without a soul. She has become estranged from her own heart and from Sissy, the child of an alternative culture, the circus, which values the imagination and emotional truth above facts and materialism. ✪ At the end of Book the First which of the themes, if any, do you think has emerged as the closest to the heart of the novel?

Let's sum up Book the First

❓ The following list covers eight key moments in Book the First but they are in alphabetical order, not the order in which they occur. Try reordering them without looking at the novel and then check your answer. Make any necessary corrections so that you end with a list in the correct order.

Bounderby's proposal of marriage is accepted by Louisa.
Drunken wife of Stephen returns to him.
Gradgrind adopts Sissy whose father has left her.
Louisa and Tom peep in at the circus.
Mrs Pegler appears outside Bounderby's house.
School life pleases Bitzer but not Sissy.
Stephen seeks advice on divorce from Bounderby.
Tom grows up and works for Bounderby.

A possible mnemonic for the correct sequence could be:
Someone **L**oses **G**old **D**uring **S**ad **M**arriage **T**o **B**ully.

? The world of *Hard Times* is filled with people from different social classes and cultural groups and Dickens wants to capture their different identities by means of their own use of language. Identify the speaker and the context for each of the quotations below and try to find for each of them another characteristic utterance that helps fix them in your imagination (names in Answers, p. 87):

(1) *They can't be alwayth a working, nor yet they can't be always a learning. Make the betht of uth; not the wortht.* (Ch. 6)

(2) *In considering this question, it is not unimportant to take into account the statistics of marriage, so far as they have yet been obtained in England and Wales.* (Ch. 15)

(3) *'One of us would be puzzled how to get old, Stephen, without t'other getting so too, both being alive,' she answered, laughing; 'but, any ways, we're such old friends, that t'hide a word of honest truth fro' one another would be a sin and a pity'.* (Ch. 10)

(4) *I passed the day in a ditch, and the night in a pigsty. That's the way I spent my tenth birthday. Not that a ditch was new to me, for I was born in a ditch.* (Ch. 10)

? Score the following statements 0–5 according to how far you agree with them (0 = completely disagree). Think of examples from the story to support your scoring.

1 Gradgrind is not so much a human character as a mouthpiece for a philosophy of education.

2 In *Hard Times* it is the circus, representing a world of imaginative sympathy, that opposes the reductionist rationalism of the education system.

3 The *Sowing* title of Book the First refers to the marriage of Louisa and Bounderby.

4 The story of Stephen, his wife and Rachel raises issues found elsewhere in the novel.

5 Whereas Sissy's nature resists the narrow conditioning of her education, Louisa falls prey to its emotional poverty and stops believing in herself.

? Draw a Mind Map with Bounderby in the centre. Round him place the characters (Louisa, Tom, Mrs Sparsit, Gradgrind, Sissy, Mrs Gradgrind). Summarize the relationship between each of them and Bounderby. Make up your own icons or copy those used in this book.

Book the Second: Reaping

Ch. 1 *Effects in the Bank*	*R̀*

◆ Mrs Sparsit talks with Bitzer in the bank.
◆ Bitzer reports on Tom's lack of progress at work.
◆ Mr Harthouse turns up looking for Bounderby.

One year has passed since the wedding of Bounderby and Louisa and the chapter opens on a hot summer's afternoon in Coketown. The town, in line with its description in Chapter 5, is described as polluted by a misty haze of soot and smoke and, in the third paragraph, weakened by legislation designed to minimize the adverse effects of its industrial way of life. The narrator ironically describes compulsory education, imposed rules to protect the workers' physical safety in the factories, and the possibility of laws prohibiting industrial pollution as instances of shocking interference in the capitalist system. ✪ Is Dickens correct in suggesting that this kind of legislation had to be forced on employers? Consult history books (or ask a history teacher) if you are unsure.

Mrs Sparsit likes to think of herself as introducing an *aristocratic* grace into the bourgeois, business atmosphere of the bank. While Bounderby represents the new wealth of the affluent middle class, founded on capitalist investment in private enterprises, Mrs Sparsit and her *Powler* connection hark back to the older aristocratic class that represented inherited wealth in Victorian Britain. Part of Bounderby's reason for retaining Mrs Sparsit is that he relishes this demonstration of the power and victory of new money over the aristocratic class it seeks to replace. Bitzer, in his talk of *uniting, and leaguing, and engaging to stand by one another*, refers to the working class and, not surprisingly, Mrs Sparsit expresses her conviction that such people *must be conquered.*

Re· Bitzer, a product of the Gradgrind philosophy, is an example of the kind of person that could be shaped by a system that prioritizes reason at the expense of emotion and the imagination. He may be *clear-headed, cautious, prudent*, but he is also the office spy who informs on colleagues, and he puts his own mother into a workhouse where he begrudges her even a supply of tea. This goes against his training, we are told, because the buying of the tea leads to no material profit. In this way we see the reason and imagination theme broadening out to include an attack on the ideology of the free market system.

Gradgrind's philosophy serves as a platform for a theory that puts material advantage above moral considerations. From a purely rational point of view, purchasing someone an annual supply of tea is of little value unless it can be sold at a higher price. Human considerations, like feelings of sympathy and obligation for an elderly mother, do not register with Bitzer and this is seen as related to the kind of education he had and the values he learnt. ✪ Can you see a connection here between Bitzer's response to his mother's situation and Louisa's response to Bounderby's proposal?

STRUCTURE

Re The opening chapter of Book 2 is one of the longest in the novel and it formed a complete episode of Dickens' serial in May 1854. Book the First, *Sowing*, began in the classroom when Sissy, Louisa, Tom and Bitzer were children and were being 'educated'. It ends some four or five years later with Louisa's young marriage. Book the Second, *Reaping*, begins after another year has passed and in Bitzer we see one result of Gradgrind's philosophy, one example of *reaping*. The introduction of a new character into the story heightens the reader's interest and there is curiosity as to what he is about. He is described as *a thorough gentleman, made to the model of the time*, and *putting no more faith in anything than Lucifer*.

Ch. 2 *Mr James Harthouse* R²

◆ Harthouse meets Bounderby and learns to flatter him.
◆ Harthouse meets Louisa and is struck by her reserve.
◆ Harthouse meets Tom but is not impressed.

Gradgrind's political party seeks an alliance with more traditional upper-class wealth as a way of securing its influence and status. A *fine gentleman* like Harthouse comes from the same class with which Mrs Sparsit has a faint family connection, though he is far more successful and financially secure. Bounderby enjoys being in a position to employ someone like her for the same reason that Gradgrind's party wishes to recruit someone like Harthouse. They seek his social kudos and envy his upper-class accent and the statement that *they pretended that they did not; but they did* would also cover Bounderby's motive in employing Mrs Sparsit. ✪ How highly regarded is an educated and/or upper-class accent now?

Harthouse's brother is an MP and Dickens describes his attitude towards a railway accident as an example of a company's indifference towards the victims of an accident for which they hold some responsibility. The same attitude, expressed in his typically stupid manner, lies behind Bounderby's introduction of Coketown to Harthouse. The polluted smoke is *the healthiest thing in the world particularly for the lungs.* ✪ Is this 'just' social criticism or do you think Dickens is linking such attitudes with the Gradgrind philosophy?

Harthouse is perceptive and intelligent, as shown by his remarkably astute judgements of Louisa and Tom and his adeptness in putting up with Bounderby. ✪ Given the way Dickens suggests character in a person's name (e.g. M'Choakumchild, Gradgrind, Bounderby), do you think anything is being suggested by the name Harthouse?

Dickens presents Harthouse as an unprincipled, aimless man, with a quick appreciation of other people's nature, and although he has done nothing reprehensible at this stage there is the suggestion that his company will not bring anything good. ✪ In the scenes where Harthouse and Louisa are together, how does Dickens suggest something unpalatable about Harthouse?

Have another look at the paragraph, about half-way through the chapter, beginning *They went out without further discourse*. Through the eyes of Harthouse, the reader sees Louisa for the first time since she married. ✪ Can you remember the last scene with Louisa and Tom at the end of Book the First, and Tom's farewell words? The incisive description of Louisa's state of mind is finely tuned and expressed through a precise choice of words: *reserved … yet watchful, constrained … yet so careless, never at a loss, and yet never at ease*.

We see Louisa after one year of married life and the result is sad and touching, the sensitive girl who speculated about life while gazing into a fire has withdrawn into a shell, *perfectly self-reliant* but vulnerable in her innocence. The reader knows how inexperienced she is – she spelled it out for her father in Chapter 15, and she is seen here trying to cope with a deeply unhappy marriage. Her essential goodness flashes into life when Tom appears and it is left to Harthouse to make a comment on this moment that serves to illustrate the lack of love in her married life. *So much the greater must have been the solitude of her heart, and her need of some one on whom to bestow it*, Harthouse observes after seeing what a *whelp* Tom Gradgrind is.

Ch. 3 *The Whelp*   *Rᶜ*

◆ Harthouse invites Tom to his room.
◆ Influenced by drink, Tom talks about his sister.

Tom Gradgrind, the whelp of the chapter's title, reveals his lack of admirable qualities in this chapter. He is not only dim-witted, foolish and gullible but selfish and callous as well, and this chapter confirms all the poor impressions the reader has received of him. ✪ What does this chapter tell us about Tom that we already knew or suspected?

Rᶜ The ironic tone of the first paragraph clearly suggests that Tom's weak character is a product of his inadequate upbringing. Three aspects of his character – hypocrisy, lack of discipline, and a weakness for *grovelling sensualities* like alcohol – are related to deficiencies in an education that marginalized imagination and self-discovery.

What is alarming about Tom is his callous lack of concern for his sister's feelings – *it was very game of her, wasn't it?* – and this lack of a moral dimension in his make-up is seen as the result of a system that values the quantifiable above the qualitative, downgrading emotional truths. The result is one very immature and irresponsible young man. In this way we see that the theme presented in the first two chapters purely within an educational context has now broadened into a more searching critique of certain values esteemed by those in a position to influence society.

STYLE AND STRUCTURE

The last paragraph ends on a disturbing note by asserting that the best thing Tom could now do would be to throw himself into the river. There is no room for humour or comic exaggeration here and Tom's gullibility points ahead, consequentially, to his sister's well-being. ✪ How does Dickens create a deadly serious tone in this paragraph? Underline or highlight the words that create an ominous sense of foreboding.

This chapter comes at the end of another weekly instalment and Dickens maintains an air of suspense by evoking a sense of dread for the future, Louisa's future in particular, but without saying how or why. At this stage in the plot Harthouse's character and motives remain unexplained and the reader is left guessing as to why Tom's conversation should be a cause for deep regret.

Before you take a break

? Draw a circle around the words below that you think describe Harthouse. Then underline one of the circled words as summing up most succinctly his moral character. Use a dictionary if necessary.

nihilistic   parasitic   paternalistic   opportunistic

supercilious   sarcastic   headstrong   hollow   vain

? Bitzer appears in Book 1, Chapters 2 and 5 and Book 2, Chapter 1. Look back at his behaviour and language in these chapters and do the same for the words below: circle those that seem applicable and underline one word that best sums him up.

callous   circumspect   solicitous   calculating

disloyal   cold-blooded   fickle   obsequious

? Now do the same for Tom and use this exercise to think about the similarities and differences between Tom and Bitzer. They are both products of the same system and while they share some characteristics they differ in other respects.

cheerful   unintelligent   canny   venal   credulous

perfidious   selfish   amoral   contemptible

Now you deserve a break.

Ch. 4 *Men and Brothers*   R²

◆ Stephen is denounced by Slackbridge at a meeting.
◆ Stephen addresses the meeting and accepts he will be ostracized.
◆ A few days later Stephen is summoned to see Bounderby.

Dickens emphasizes Stephen's working-class identity both in the content of what he says to his fellow workers and in the way he says it. It is significant that Slackbridge does not speak like a working man, as if to suggest that he does not share the social world of those he claims to represent.

An example of the way in which the novel's themes sometimes overlap and reinforce one another can be seen here in the way the themes of goodness and capitalism feed into the portrayal of Stephen and his fellow workers. Both Stephen and the workers he addresses are presented as essentially good people who struggle to maintain their honesty and dignity in the face of unhelpful circumstances.

There is a keenly felt sense of solidarity amongst the workers, based on their shared understanding that the conditions of their working lives should and could be improved. Every worker, we are told, *felt his only hope to be in his allying himself to the comrades by whom he was surrounded* and it is this willingness to recognize the need for concerted action that Slackbridge is able to exploit to poor Stephen's disadvantage. The mill workers have an awareness of the need for united, political action and Dickens points out, in the long sentence at the end of the fourth paragraph, that being manipulated by Slackbridge does not diminish the justness of their complaints against their conditions of work.

LANGUAGE

Dickens stresses Stephen's working-class, northern-English manner of speaking by introducing dialect words, like *moydert* (confused), *hetter* (heated), *fratch* (quarrel), words written phonetically to capture the way they are pronounced, like *Gonnows* (God knows), *o'* (of), *heer* (here), and *mun* (must), and grammatical non-standard English expressions like *I were*, meaning I was. ○ Which other characters in the novel speak with their own distinctive voices? An important difference underlying the language of Stephen and that of Sleary, whom you may have thought of in response to the last question, is that Stephen's speech is typical of his social class in that part of England, whereas Sleary's speech is characterized by his idiosyncratic inability to pronounce certain sounds. Do you think Dickens is more successful in rendering Stephen's manner of speaking than he is with the rendering of Sleary's speech? If so, why do you think this might be so?

The characterization of Slackbridge has been criticized on the grounds that no union leader at the time would actually have spoken in the way he does. This has been disputed by other critics. What can be certain is that Slackbridge is to be seen as manipulative and lacking in integrity and the falseness of his character is revealed through his bombastic language. It is made more apparent by Dickens simply stating this to be the case, rather than evoking it through imaginative use of language.

STYLE AND STRUCTURE

The fact that Slackbridge does not talk like Stephen has already been noted and in his loud manner, his bullying air of conviction and his practised theatricality (he is observed, *wiping his hot forehead – always from left to right, and never the reverse way*, as if this is a rhetorical gesture), he more resembles Bounderby than any other character in the novel. Dickens also describes him in such a way as to suggest the poverty of his moral nature.

Slackbridge is the last new character to be introduced into the novel and he brings with him another development of the subplot involving Stephen and one that will later impinge on the main plot through the actions of Tom and others.

Ch. 5 *Men and Masters* ℞

◆ Bounderby unsuccessfully quizzes Stephen about the trade union.
◆ Stephen defends the workers and annoys Bounderby, who sacks him.
◆ Louisa, Tom and Harthouse are all present in the background.

This is the most political chapter in the book and directly addresses the state of social and industrial relations in Britain, a *muddle* as Stephen calls it. As the chapter title indicates, the division between the social classes expresses itself in the poor state of relations between employers and workers. Stephen unhesitatingly identifies himself with his fellow workers and he feels compelled to speak up for them by the *proud consciousness that he was faithful to his class*. Bounderby also sees himself as a representative employer, using the first-person plural when exclaiming that *we will make an example* by using the law to defeat union action.

The treatment of social class in *Hard Times* is bound up with the economic system of capitalism and the heart of the disagreement between Bounderby and Stephen revolves around the desired nature of society. Stephen, in the paragraph beginning *Sir, I were never good at showin' o't*, asks his employer to consider the alienation of working-class life and the monotony of their lives. He goes on to reject the use of state power to coerce workers, *The strong hand will never do't*, or the simple application of free market economics, *Nor yet lettin' alone will never do't*. This is another polemical passage where the reader may sense Dickens speaking through the character of Stephen.

R² The reason and imagination theme makes a sudden contribution to Stephen's argument as he pleads for an end to *reg'latin* people *as if they was figures in a soom, or machines; wi'out loves and likens, wi'out memories and inclinations, wi'out souls to weary and souls to hope.* The argument touches a nerve with Bounderby, who interrupts him to terminate his employment.

STRUCTURE

Louisa plays a silent but significant role in this chapter. Stephen finds himself instinctively wishing to direct his remarks at her and it is the cause of some exasperation on Bounderby's part that he is ignored by his employee, and at a critical point in the scene he detects an eye movement on her part, gesturing towards the door. This comes just after the point where Stephen has rebuffed Bounderby's threat of transporting leaders with the analogy of transporting a clock to Norfolk Island in the Pacific. Time will still go on, he says, and even Bounderby might have felt the simple logic of this argument. Louisa glances at the door, as if willing Stephen to leave while he still has a job, but Stephen stands holding the door handle and delivers a final verbal assault on Bounderby and the unequal society that he embodies.

Behind the human interest of this momentary encounter between Stephen and Louisa, an important shift has occurred in the structure of the plot. Up until now, the story of the Gradgrind and Bounderby nexus has been separated, at the plot level, from the story of Stephen and Rachel and their way of life. Here, the hint that Louisa's feelings have been aroused by Stephen is the beginning of a drawing together of the two stories. Remember, Tom and Harthouse are also in the room and they are also affected by what takes place.

Ch. 6 *Fading Away* $R\ell$

◆ Stephen meets Mrs Pegler and Rachel and they have tea together.
◆ Louisa, accompanied by Tom, arrives at his lodging place hoping to help.
◆ Tom privately arranges for Stephen to wait for a message outside the bank.
◆ Stephen leaves Coketown.

Stephen's act of goodness, by instinctively thinking of how his dismissal will protect Rachel from recrimination, complements the more momentous import of Louisa's decision to help Stephen. ❂ Why is Louisa's selflessness more significant than Stephen's act of also thinking of someone else?

Part of the quality of Louisa's act of goodness in seeking out Stephen lies in the fact that she crosses a social divide to reach out to him. We are told that this is the first time she has ever been inside a working person's home and her compassionate and respectful behaviour arises from her own awareness of this. Dickens becomes more explicit about the class divisions in society, in the paragraph that follows the farewell between Stephen and Rachel, when he warns of social revolution looming ahead. A violent fracturing of society is envisaged, *reality will take a wolfish turn, and make an end of you*, unless a change of heart takes place in relations between the employed and the employers.

$R\ell$ Earlier in the chapter, in the paragraph following Louisa's appearance at Stephen's lodging, capitalism is criticized for treating people as merely an investment, *something wholesale, of which vast fortunes were made*, for their humanity is diluted by being classified as just a tool of production. The Gradgrind philosophy classifies people as mere statistical groups and class conflict will intensify *when romance is entirely driven out of their souls*.

Although this is a relatively long chapter, these ideas are expressed in a compressed form and their force comes from relating the ideas to the characters in the story. It is worth reading the chapter again, pausing after each point where the author seems to be speaking and relating the general point to characters and events in the novel.

STYLE AND LANGUAGE

Hard Times can be called a rhetorical novel in the sense that there is no mistaking the polemical tone of voice of the author. One of the strongest expressions of Dickens' own voice comes in the paragraph after Stephen's and Rachel's farewell. There is a note of contempt and even anger in expressions like *gabblers of many little dog's-eared creeds* and *genteel and used-up infidels*. ○ Which character do you think this last expression could describe? Can you find another example in the novel where the author makes himself heard?

STRUCTURE

This chapter appeared as a separate instalment, as did also the following two chapters, and one can see why. Structurally, it marks a pivotal episode in the plot by bringing together characters from the two storylines that have been running along their own lines up until now. The previous chapter, as we saw on page 64, brought Stephen and Louisa in the same room and now they meet to talk, bringing Louisa and Rachel together for the first time. Tom also becomes involved because of his plan to exploit Stephen for his own ends.

From the reader's perspective, this is a dramatic chapter that hints at future developments but leaves the reader guessing as to how the story will unfold. Strangely, for such a proactive chapter, the title is *Fading Away*. ○ What do you think the title is referring to?

This chapter explains that Rachel urged Stephen *to avoid trouble* and his promise to do so is what lay behind his refusal to join the union. ○ Do you find this a convincing explanation? It seems a structural weakness in the sense that Stephen is getting into trouble because of his promise, a promise that had the intention of avoiding trouble! It would be easy to imagine someone sensible like Rachel at least trying to talk him out of it, but it is equally easy to see how the plot as a whole moves forward significantly by making Stephen an outcast who gets the sack. Stephen's promise is the novelist's weak explanation for initiating this plot development.

A little bit of work to do

? Write down the following sentences spoken by Stephen in standard English, the way you would imagine them being spoken by someone reading the news on television: *Monny's the pleasant word as soom heer has spok'n wi' me; monny's the face I see heer, as I first seen when I were young and lighter heart'n than now. I ha' never had no fratch afore, sin ever I were born, wi' any o' my like; Gonnows I ha' none now that's of my makin'.*

? A popular radio show, *Just a Minute*, challenges guests to speak on a subject for one minute without repetition, hesitation, or deviation from the subject. You can try this on your own but it is more fun with a partner, who need not necessarily know the novel. Here are two subjects to talk on: (a) What does Stephen say is wrong with Bounderby's attitude to working people? (b) A summary of what happens to Stephen from his appearance at the union meeting to his leaving Coketown.

? Think about the differences between Bounderby and Stephen and for each topic below write down the first response they might give.

> The secret of success
> A motto
> Good things about life
> Regrets
> Favourite sports team
> The meaning of life

Take a break – then come back with a bang!

Ch. 7 *Gunpowder* $R^?$

◆ Louisa and Bounderby live in a new house where Harthouse is a frequent visitor.
◆ Tom, who owes people money, thinks Harthouse is his friend.
◆ Harthouse plans to win Louisa's heart through Tom.

This chapter traces an important development in the relationship between Louisa and Harthouse, one that is handled with convincing psychological insight by Dickens. ✪ Can you identify the two ways by which Louisa is drawn into Harthouse's confidence in this chapter? An underlying reason for Harthouse's success is that he is able to tap into her feelings of emotional isolation and her sense that life is meaningless.

$R^?$ · Louisa's upbringing, which has led to her loveless marriage, makes her susceptible to Harthouse's claim that there are no values worth believing in. His profession of ethical nihilism *came as a relief and justification* to Louisa for *everything being hollow and worthless, she had missed nothing and sacrificed nothing.* ✪ Can you recall what phrase she repeated to herself, when her father was outlining the proposal of marriage, that expressed her sense of life's worthlessness? Harthouse's adult philosophy endorses how she was brought up to feel about life, for her strictly rationalist upbringing left no space for moral values, and the fourth paragraph finds her repeating the phrase from Book 1, Chapter 15.

What makes Louisa an interesting character is that there is more to her than this. Her *struggling disposition* to believe in human goodness accounts for her ever agreeing to marry Bounderby in the first place and in the last chapter the same charitable impulse brought her to Stephen's lodgings with a desire to help him. The second reason for Harthouse's success in bringing himself close to Louisa is his canny duplicity in convincing her that he really cares for Tom and his predicament. Even Tom is touched by this show of apparent benevolence in the scene that takes place between them in the garden, at a spot where Harthouse knows they can be seen from Louisa's bedroom.

Notice also how Harthouse is able to play on the fact that her husband's character does not offer any avenue of hope when it comes to helping Tom. ❂ How does Louisa's acute embarrassment over her husband reveal itself in conversation with Harthouse?

Bounderby's new house has been purchased, presumably at a bargain price, after the failure of its original owner to pay the mortgage. Bounderby's occupation of the house provides him with more opportunities to display his inverted snobbery, by pretending to despise what he secretly craves. ❂ Explain in your own words how his story about Nickits' paintings is his way of demonstrating social superiority. Bounderby's ugly and malicious character is tellingly revealed by the enjoyment with which he recounts the sad reversal of Nickits' fortunes. Bounderby may have a large house in the country, away from the squalor of Coketown, but his social success depends on the misfortunes of others and the exploitation of working-class people like Stephen.

This chapter skilfully binds the personal with the political and brings together a number of themes which are now beginning to overlap more than ever before. ❂ Why do you think this chapter is entitled *Gunpowder*?

Ch. 8 *Explosion* R'

♦ Harthouse is informed of the bank robbery.
♦ Stephen Blackpool is suspected.
♦ Mrs Sparsit is invited to stay at the Bounderby house.

The third and fourth paragraphs of the chapter also dwell on the nature of Harthouse's wickedness by stressing the fact that he is not an evil person in the sense of a self-conscious villain who maliciously plots the downfall of someone innocent.

The threat to goodness comes not from a malevolent villain but from the state of mind that Harthouse embodies. His lack of moral values, his inability to feel much sense of ethical behaviour, is what makes him so dangerous. Dickens employs the metaphor of floating icebergs to express the moral danger that people like Harthouse represent. ❂ Do you think that people like this are the real villains of the modern world?

The chapter begins with Harthouse congratulating himself on the progress he has made in his relationship with Louisa. He is very aware that he is only able to get close to Louisa because of her loveless marriage to Bounderby. Mrs Sparsit is equally astute at recognizing Louisa's indifference towards her husband. Her repeated 'mistake' of calling Louisa Miss Gradgrind rather than Mrs Bounderby, her invitation to Bounderby to play backgammon and to prepare his favourite late-night drink are all calculated ploys aimed at destabilizing their marriage and planting seeds of doubt in Bounderby's mind.

STRUCTURE

The author's skill in managing the plot of the novel is very apparent in this chapter. The previous hints (see the two 'Structure' paragraphs above) that the story of Stephen Blackpool, and that of the mysterious old woman known as Mrs Pegler, will interact with the main plot featuring the Bounderby and Gradgrind families are now realized through the mechanism of the bank robbery. Louisa, Bounderby, Harthouse, Tom, Blackpool, Mrs Sparsit and Mrs Pegler are now all involved in the robbery incident, and by bringing Mrs Sparsit to stay at the Bounderby home there is more scope for Dickens to work at unifying the plot. Like the two previous chapters, this chapter appeared as a separate weekly instalment. By the end of it the reader can see how the plot is moving towards a conclusion. There is little doubt but that Tom is responsible for the robbery, and that Louisa strongly suspects this, and the chapter ends on a note of anticipation as to how the plot will now develop. ✪ Can you spot it?

Ch. 9 *Hearing the Last of it*   R²

◆ Bounderby's composure is unsettled at the breakfast table.
◆ Louisa returns to Stone Lodge to visit her dying mother.

Mrs Sparsit's sly tactics, aimed at re-establishing her intimacy with Bounderby and isolating Louisa, are beginning to bear some fruit. Her pampering of Bounderby is cleverly designed to remind him just how little interest his wife shows in his welfare, and his ruffled composure reveals itself at the breakfast table.

Mrs Sparsit's conversation with Harthouse, before Bounderby appears, also shows her sharp awareness of the relationship developing between Louisa and him. The authorial voice informs the reader that the incident at the breakfast table was one more stage in the weakening of the husband-and-wife bond while concomitantly strengthening a growing alliance between Louisa and Harthouse.

Louisa's return home, a rare occurrence since her marriage, gives rise to a long paragraph in the middle of the chapter, beginning *Neither, as she approached her old home now*, that evokes the pathos of her unhappy childhood.

R? She has no happy memories of the kind that Dickens says are so important to the emotional and social health of adult life. ✪ Underline phrases and words in the paragraph where Dickens expresses the importance of a happy childhood that balances reason with the claims of the imagination.

The overlap of the parental theme with that of reason and imagination emerges in the deathbed scene between Louisa and Mrs Gradgrind. The poignancy of Mrs Gradgrind's surprise that anyone should want to hear about her reminds us of Gradgrind's domineering role in the family and her enigmatic observation that *there's a pain somewhere in the room … but I couldn't positively say that I have got it* brings us to the heart of Gradgrind's inadequacy as a parent. In her dying moments, Mrs Gradgrind speaks of something, *not an Ology at all – that your father has missed.* ✪ Write down what you think Mrs Gradgrind wanted to put down on paper for the benefit of her husband.

LANGUAGE, STYLE AND STRUCTURE

The characterization of Mrs Sparsit has always been associated with imagery suggesting a bird of prey and this approach is further developed here. The way in which her predatory nature works has been seen in the previous chapter as well as this one and Dickens captures her ability to mask vindictiveness behind a show of manners in the startling image that brings the first paragraph to an end. The villains of *Hard Times* are not grim criminals, of the kind that Bounderby is representing Blackpool to be, but smooth and polished characters like Harthouse and Mrs Sparsit. ✪ Look through some recent newspapers and find some contemporary examples of polished villains like Harthouse and Mrs Sparsit.

Louisa's visit home to see her dying mother serves two important purposes in the structure of the novel. It brings Sissy back into the story and prepares the ground for a development of her role in the unfolding events. It also serves to remind the reader of the significant moment that occurred at the end of Book 1, Chapter 15. ❂ Look back at that chapter and remind yourself of Louisa's state of mind at the time she accepted Bounderby's proposal of marriage.

Ch. 10 *Mrs Sparsit's Staircase* *Rʑ*

◆ Mrs Sparsit contemplates Louisa's descent into shame.
◆ Louisa and Harthouse discuss the bank robbery.

The metaphor of a staircase *with a dark pit of shame and ruin at the bottom,* down which Mrs Sparsit sees Louisa descending, expresses the woman's conviction that the Bounderby marriage will succumb to adultery. Mrs Sparsit's relishing of the prospect is convincing, and takes us back to the last chapter of Book 1, where Bounderby announced his forthcoming marriage and Mrs Sparsit received the news with repressed malice. ❂ Look back to the previous chapter and identify a conversation that prepares the reader for the way Mrs Sparsit's thinking is revealed in this chapter. Louisa's conversation with Harthouse in this chapter shows Harthouse continuing to worm his way into her affections through Tom.

LANGUAGE, STYLE AND STRUCTURE

This short chapter confirms Mrs Sparsit's developing role in the plot. Bounderby's invitation for her to stay over the weekends at his house makes it clear that she will be involved in future events. Both of the two conversations that occupy this chapter remind the reader of the bank robbery and its continuing significance for the plot, even though there are no new developments.

The staircase metaphor is not the only example in this chapter of Dickens' use of imagery to encapsulate aspects of character. Mrs Sparsit, intuitively aware of their growing intimacy, looks forward to their adultery and at the end of the chapter this expectation on her part is expressed through a harvesting image. ❂ Underline the sentence that expresses this idea. Does the image remind you of a similar metaphor that has been at work in the novel as a whole? For Mrs Sparsit the collapse of Louisa's marriage will represent the ripeness and fullness of the harvest, and the novel as a whole is structured by a farming calendar division into sowing, reaping and garnering. Mrs Sparsit looks to the future for what she sees as an inevitable conclusion to present events and the reader is also led forward to contemplate this possible outcome. At the same time, the reader is left wondering what conclusion there will be to other events like the bank robbery and what resolution there will be to the various themes that are at work in the book.

Ch. 11 *Lower and Lower* Rε͏ˈ

◆ Mrs Sparsit's spying convinces her that Louisa and Harthouse are about to commit adultery.
◆ Harthouse declares his love to Louisa in the rain, secretly watched by Mrs Sparsit.
◆ Louisa is followed back to Coketown by Mrs Sparsit, where she loses sight of her.

The theme of marriage in the novel takes on a serious and adult complexion as Harthouse, exploiting the opportunity offered by Bounderby's absence, makes his move and declares his intentions to Louisa. In terms of psychological conviction the scene has been effectively prepared for because Harthouse's behaviour is consistent with his moral nihilism, and the hollow boredom of his life makes an affair with Louisa seem a diverting amusement. The loveless state of Louisa's own marriage, her loneliness and her need for affection, make it possible that she will succumb to Harthouse's attempted seduction.

LANGUAGE, STYLE AND STRUCTURE

The staircase metaphor binds together the last three chapters of Book 2, by means of the chapters' titles and by references within the text. Chapter 11 begins by employing the image to suggest that Louisa's descent into adultery is only a matter of time, and Mrs Sparsit's anticipation of what is about to happen suddenly becomes creditable when the reader realizes that Tom has indeed been sent to the station by Harthouse as a ploy to keep him out of the way. The style of this chapter, with its fast pace, unfolding surprises and exciting developments, engages the reader's attention in the same way that a thriller or detective story would. As the chapter draws to an end the reader is left guessing as to Louisa's motives and intentions.

The **melodrama** (sensational drama appealing to the emotions) that characterizes this chapter can also be seen in the way Dickens injects a downpour of sudden rain at the climactic moment. The heavy rain, a secret meeting in the woods, sexual angst, and the sinister voyeurism of Mrs Sparsit, combine to create a *film noir* atmosphere of suppressed desire that has not been seen in the book up till now.

Mrs Sparsit, no longer a mere parody of the social class system, has emerged as an obsessive predator who wills the adultery to happen with a suppressed passion of her own. There is a brilliant description of her watching Louisa leave the wood for the house, nine paragraphs from the end of the chapter, that portrays her as a witch-like obsessive. Suddenly, all her social pretensions are stripped away and her real nature exposed.

A similar effect is at work in the chapter's final paragraph where this paragon of bourgeois virtue and sobriety is exposed by her exertions as someone very ugly indeed, both literally and metaphorically. ❂ Underline the words and phrases in these two paragraphs that convey this highly unpalatable impression of Mrs Sparsit.

Ch. 12 *Down* $R\iota^{\cdot}$

◆ Mr Gradgrind is visited by a highly distraught Louisa.
◆ Louisa, after telling him of Harthouse's proposal, collapses on the ground.

$R\iota^{\cdot}$ In this chapter we see the merging of the two themes of marriage and reason and the imagination. Louisa, highly charged and on the verge of a nervous breakdown, spells out the effect on her mind of an upbringing that denied the role of imagination and creative independence and which provided her with no sense of emotional security. *What you have never nurtured in me, you have never nurtured in yourself.* ❂ What do you think Louisa means by this statement? Is she accusing Gradgrind of repressing his own emotional nature and thus denying love to both of them? Is Gradgrind solely to blame for the miserable childhood of his daughter, or are we to view Gradgrind himself as a victim?

When Gradgrind and his system were first presented, at the beginning of the first book, the element of parody and exaggeration took precedence but now we see the dreadful human cost of the way he has brought up his children. Louisa argues that the lack of an outlet for her imagination has made her a loveless and unhappy woman and, although she does not employ psychological terms such as 'guilt' or 'repression', that her anxiety to deny this side of her nature has almost destroyed her moral being. *I have almost repulsed and crushed my better angel into a demon*, she says, when explaining why she accepted marriage to Bounderby and, by implication, why she has almost succumbed to Harthouse's advances.

LANGUAGE, STYLE AND STRUCTURE

The concluding chapter to the second book is highly theatrical and although, considering her deeply troubled state of mind, the style of Louisa's address to her father is highly unrealistic, there is no mistaking the dramatic force of the last sentence. *And he laid her down there, and saw the pride of his heart and the triumph of his system, lying, an insensible heap, at his feet.* Its dramatic impetus and significance derives from its structural role in the novel, for this is the final statement and the final scene of the second book, entitled *Reaping*, and the force of the farming metaphor that structures the novel as a whole is brought to bear on the silent figure of Louisa lying at her father's feet. Gradgrind's philosophy was applied to the life of a child; the broken woman, unconscious in her grief, is the result of this nurture.

Time to take stock

? As a character, Louisa changes and develops more than anyone else in the novel and, as she explains to her father, she has always been torn by the conflict between her own inner needs and the dictates of her ultrarational upbringing. In each of the boxes below, identify a scene in the novel where we have witnessed this conflict within her own self. One of the boxes has been filled in as an example.

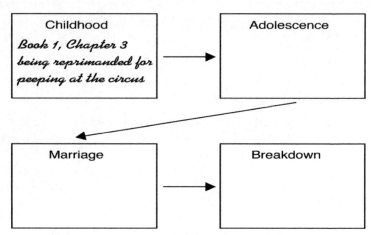

? Draw a Mind Map with Louisa in the centre and place round her the characters of Gradgrind, Tom, Mrs Sparsit, Bounderby and Harthouse. Summarize for each character their attitude towards Louisa. Add another branch for Gradgrind's attitude after the scene at the end of the second book.

? Draw a pie chart that includes the characters of Louisa, Tom and Gradgrind and divide the pie to reflect the amount of sympathy you feel for each character.

? Draw a countdown clock for Stephen Blackpool, inserting each incident that contributes to the general feeling that he is responsible for the bank robbery.

Book the Third: Garnering

Ch. 1 *Another Thing Needful*

◆ Louisa recuperates and is visited by her humbled father.
◆ Sissy and Louisa become friends.

Gradgrind accepts responsibility for his failure as a parent and as a proponent of a narrow philosophy that he now sees to be woefully inadequate. His only excuse is that he meant well, something that Louisa knows to be true, and there is a touching scene *as he softly moved her scattered hair from her forehead with his hand.* Such moments of intimacy, coming from a parent who is only now realizing his lack of contact with his daughter, physically and emotionally, help make convincing the development of his character from a figure of fun and parody to someone deserving pity.

Re Gradgrind expresses his understanding of the importance of imagination and the limitations of pure reason in terms of *wisdom of the Head* and *wisdom of the Heart* and he now senses that the *instinct that is wanted* is not something quantifiable, it is not something that can be defined like Bitzer's exposition of what is a horse, and that it comes from within the individual. Gradgrind's realization of this comes most dramatically from the return of the broken Louisa to his home and it helps him to clarify his sense of what Sissy has brought to their family. ○ Identify and underline the sentence where Gradgrind tries to tell his daughter this.

The relationship between Louisa and Sissy undergoes an important development in this chapter and it is handled with psychological insight. ○ Look back to Chapter 15 in the first book to remind yourself of how far they had grown apart. Louisa turned against Sissy because Sissy's response to hearing of the marriage to Bounderby registered Louisa's own deepest regrets. Blocking out Sissy from her life was one way of repressing her own anxieties, but *all closely imprisoned forces rend and destroy* and Louisa now struggles with the consequences of her denial. It has caused her pain and turmoil but she cannot just shrug it off and regain emotional and mental health in an instant. Louisa is initially reluctant to accept Sissy because to do so means being honest with herself and coming to terms with the kind of person she has allowed herself to become. More than once in this chapter the reader is made aware of Louisa's difficulty in facing up to Sissy. The first two occasions occur early on, in the conversation between Louisa and her young sister Jane, where the mention of Sissy's name causes Louisa to react negatively, and there is a suggestion of it in her conversation with Gradgrind when he hints at Sissy's therapeutic presence in the house and Louisa *made him no reply.*

✒ STRUCTURE

The title of this chapter echoes the opening chapter of the novel, entitled *The One Thing Needful*, and serves as a commentary upon what has happened since the story began. The title of this third and final book, *Garnering*, refers to the collecting and storing of the harvest's crop and in terms of the novel's themes this can be seen as representing the consequences and resolution to some of the ideas that have been explored. Louisa's breakdown represents the failure of the philosophy that shaped her education and upbringing, though it also offers hope in the form of reconciliation with her father and Sissy. The novel's structure leads the reader to expect more consequences and resolutions to arise from what has gone before.

Ch. 2 *Very Ridiculous*   *R²*

◆ Puzzled, Harthouse waits to find out what has happened.
◆ Sissy visits Harthouse and he subsequently leaves Coketown.

The validity of F.R. Leavis' description of the novel as a 'moral fable' (see 'Critical approaches') is apparent in this chapter and it weakens the force of the criticism that this encounter between Harthouse and Sissy is unconvincing in terms of psychology and character. Although there is a psychological complexity in the novel, in the portrayal of Louisa for instance, Sissy's role is more symbolic because she represents the force of goodness. ✪ Is it believable that someone like Harthouse, realizing that his attempt to seduce a woman with whom he is not passionately in love has failed, would capitulate like this? Perhaps the reader's credulity is stretched by Harthouse's agreement to leave Coketown, *immediately and finally*, but in terms of a moral fable the act is necessary.

Sissy's goodness is a given fact, and Dickens describes her encounter with Harthouse as a victory of goodness over mendacity and immorality. Look, for example, at the paragraph beginning *Mr Harthouse drew a long breath.* ✪ Do you find yourself accepting her decisive victory over Harthouse? Remembering, too, how Harthouse has been presented – a bored young man with more money than sense, lacking moral integrity, but not an evil monster – you may find yourself understanding his discomfort before Sissy and his shallow sense of shame at having failed so miserably in his attempt to seduce Louisa.

Ch. 3 *Very Decided* *R?*

◆ Mrs Sparsit finds Bounderby in London and tells him about Harthouse and Louisa.
◆ Bounderby returns to Coketown where a period of separation between him and his wife is suggested by Gradgrind.
◆ When Louisa fails to meet Bounderby's ultimatum he returns her belongings to Gradgrind's home and puts his own country house up for sale.

STRUCTURE

Some of the themes in the novel are approaching their resolution or, in terms of the farming image that structures the novel as a whole, some *garnering* is now taking place. Mrs Sparsit's role is almost but not quite over, for the chapter is more concerned with the breakdown of Bounderby's marriage.

Towards the end of the chapter Dickens draws attention to a parallel between the breakdown in Stephen Blackpool's marriage and that of Bounderby and Louisa. ❍ Look back to Book 1, Chapter 10 and find some words of Bounderby's that illustrate his hypocrisy.

Unlike Bounderby, Gradgrind has learned a lot from what has happened and the chapter confirms our impression of him as an essentially caring parent who is trying to make the best of a situation for which he accepts a lot of the responsibility.

Ch. 4 *Lost* *R?*

◆ Bounderby publicly implicates Stephen Blackpool in the bank robbery.
◆ Rachel, Bounderby and Tom visit the Gradgrinds to confirm

Rachel's account of what happened the night before
Stephen left Coketown.

◆ Rachel writes to Stephen but he fails to return to defend
himself against the charges.

LANGUAGE AND STRUCTURE

The narrative pace quickens as we return to the bank robbery
but Dickens is not yet ready to resolve the plot. The reader's
interest is engaged by the mystery of Stephen's whereabouts,
as is the interest of Tom Gradgrind for quite a different reason.
The conversation between Gradgrind and his daughter over
Stephen's character is rich with irony as he wonders where
and who the real culprit is. ❂ Why do you think Sissy flushes
when she meets Louisa's eyes and why does Louisa put her
finger on her lips?

Rachel's defence of Stephen raises again the theme of
social class in the novel and Dickens also returns to his
criticism of trade union leaders like Slackbridge.

At the beginning of the chapter Bounderby is compared to
Venus, the Roman goddess of love and beauty whom the
Greeks called Aphrodite. In Greek myth she was born fully
formed out of the sea, but Dickens has Bounderby rising from
the mud as a self-made entrepreneur. This is a bizarre yet
appropriate image, since Bounderby's account of his own
origins will also turn out to be mythical.

Ch. 5 *Found*

◆ Rachel and Sissy discuss nightly the whereabouts of Stephen.
◆ Mrs Sparsit finds Mrs Pegler and brings her to Bounderby's
home.

Dickens maintains narrative suspense in a chapter
entitled *Found* by tidying up the mystery of Mrs Pegler
rather than the central mystery of Stephen's whereabouts. The
exposure of Bounderby, which reveals him to be the ungrateful
son of a loving mother, takes place not just in the company of
his acquaintances but with a cross-section of Coketown's
general public also present. This ensures maximum publicity
for the true story of his parentage: his humiliation is complete.

Sissy's essential goodness is shown by her nightly attendance at Rachel's lodging and this, along with Rachel's complete faith in Stephen, helps create a moral symmetry in a chapter that begins with their goodness and faith in human nature and ends with the exposure of Bounderby's perfidy, the defeat of the obnoxious Mrs Sparsit and the lurking presence of Tom Gradgrind.

Ch. 6 *The Starlight*

- Sissy and Rachel discover the fatally injured Stephen.
- Gradgrind is asked by him to speak to his son and clear his name.
- Stephen dies as he is being brought back to Coketown.

The manner of Stephen Blackpool's accident and death is not only important in terms of the novel's plot. Dickens prepares the reader for its social and political significance by beginning the chapter with a description of the way Britain's industrial revolution has scarred the countryside with coal pits and spent coal mines. People may leave Coketown for a Sunday stroll in the countryside to forget the grimness of their working environment but there is no real escape from their industrial world.

In his dying words Stephen dwells on the painful irony that a coal shaft that killed so many workers when it was operating continues to kill when it is closed down (*fire-damp* refers to carburetted hydrogen, a common source of explosions in coal mines). In his goodness Stephen thinks not of himself but of Rachel's young sister who died young, a victim of a cruel society that placed profits before people. He calls for mutual understanding between the social classes as the only means of resolving *the muddle*.
❂ How are the working class represented in this chapter?

LANGUAGE, STYLE AND STRUCTURE

This chapter is rich in symbolism, beginning and ending with scenes of natural light, and associating the death of a good man with the social evil of industrial capitalism as represented by *Old Hell Shaft*. The mystery of Stephen's whereabouts is explained for the reader and the dying man's plea to

Gradgrind to speak with his son makes clear Tom Gradgrind will not escape responsibility for what has happened. ✪ How do you feel about the way Dickens handles Stephen's death? Is it too sentimental or do you find the symbolism dignified and moving?

Ch. 7 *Whelp-Hunting*   *Rᶤ*

◆ Sissy instructs Tom to escape to Sleary's circus.
◆ Gradgrind, and Sissy and Louisa, journey separately to see Tom.
◆ Tom's escape abroad is organized but Bitzer turns up intent on preventing it.

Rᶤ Chapter 7 is rich in irony, not least of which is the way Gradgrind now finds himself relying on the circus to effect his son's escape. The reason and imagination theme takes another ironic turn when Tom points out to his father that, by the law of averages he was so fond of quoting, it should not surprise him to learn that someone has dishonestly abused their position of trust. The theme merges seamlessly with the theme of parents. The sad failure of Gradgrind both as a parent and as a practitioner of an inadequate system of education is apparent in Tom's abject remark, *I can't be more miserable anywhere … than I have been here, ever since I can remember.*

LANGUAGE, STYLE AND STRUCTURE

Rᶤ Sleary's reappearance, and his distinctive manner of speaking, remind us of the symbolic importance of the circus and another layer of symbolism is added by the visual spectacle of Tom's comic disguise: *And one of his model children had come to this!*

Chapter 7 began the final instalment appearing in *Household Words* in 1854 and Dickens maintains the dramatic pace to the very end. Sissy's essential goodness is counterbalanced by the essential nastiness of Bitzer, whose surprise arrival at the end of Chapter 7 adds a new note of drama and tension to the plot.

Ch. 8 *Philosophical* $R\acute{e}$

◆ Bitzer explains and defends his reasons for apprehending Tom.

◆ Tom's escape is engineered by Sleary with the help of his circus animals.

◆ Sleary expounds his own philosophy to Gradgrind.

$R\acute{e}$ · The irony in Chapter 8 takes a painful turn as Gradgrind tries to appeal to Bitzer on the grounds of compassion only to find his appeal rejected by the *catechism* of reason and pragmatism that he so ably taught Bitzer.

The Gradgrind philosophy of self-interest is seen to underpin a social system that reduces everything to the level of the free market, *a bargain across a counter,* and where even heaven could be imagined as some kind of privatized *politico-economical place.* An alternative to the ethics of capitalism is evoked by Sleary when he speaks of a way of life that is based not on self-interest but on *thomething very different; t'other, that it hath a way of ith own of calculating or not calculating.*

LANGUAGE, STYLE AND STRUCTURE

Chapter 8 lives up to its name as it deconstructs the dominant philosophy of the modern world, arguing that self-interest and the law of the market work against other forces in human nature that are equally valid as a basis for political and economic life. Dickens is writing imaginative fiction, not a work of political philosophy, so he does not express this in the language of political discourse. The style that Dickens does adopt illustrates his fundamental point that an alternative to the world that Bitzer inhabits must depend upon an appeal to the heart and to qualities that rely on imagination and empathy rather than reason and self-interest. This is the significance of Sleary, who helps Tom escape. He does so out of compassion and gratitude to Gradgrind. The escape stratagem is effected in a wonderfully fantastical manner involving dancing horses and an intelligent dog. Horses and dogs, of course, return the reader to the classroom lectures in the early chapters of the book and this adds a delightful and symbolic touch to the escape.

Sleary also clears up the question of what happened to Sissy's father by confirming he must have died.

Ch. 9 *Final* *Rͤ*

◆ Mrs Sparsit is packed off to Lady Scadgers by Bounderby.
◆ A glimpse into the future lives of most of the characters is provided.
◆ Readers are urged to act like the good characters.

Rͤ All the themes are touched on in the final chapter. The limitations of reason and the importance of imaginative and humane qualities characterize the future lives of good people like Rachel and Sissy. The warmth of Sissy's future family life comes from her happy marriage, her role as a loving parent and as someone who does not turn her back on the working class. Like Gradgrind, she grows to see and feel that happiness for all depends on human values rather than the grim logic of industrial capitalism.

This is a positive reading of the last chapter's glimpse into the future. A more melancholy reading sees the Gradgrind family surviving only in a very fractured way. Tom is forced to live abroad and although he does repent he dies alone. Gradgrind is a broken and powerless man who is ridiculed in the parliament he once had such faith in, and Louisa never enjoys a family of her own. The Gradgrinds as a family only survive in a private sphere and cannot function as a model for a healthier society. It is Bounderby who survives with his economic power not only undiminished but extended due to his will, which creates a new breed of *five-and-twenty Humbugs … each taking upon himself the name, Josiah Bounderby of Coketown … supported out of a Bounderby estate.*

The inadequacies in family relationships that the novel has revealed can be seen to seriously weaken the idea that any social progress has been made. Rachel still has to toil in Bounderby's mill and, while Sissy offers some hope, there is no suggestion that society has been transformed.

Rͤ The final paragraph talks of our two fields of action, the personal values of compassion nurtured by the imaginative faculty, and the public world where people can socially interact on a humane level as a matter of duty. This is an affirmative statement but it is more a wish than anything else and there is no conviction that the personal and the public spheres can merge and transform society. We can do our moral duty and try to be better people, Dickens seems to be saying, but society as a whole remains unchanged.

✪ What is your opinion about the tone of the final few chapters? Do you find it uplifting and positive or melancholy and resigned?

Looking back

? The illustrations on p. 86 represent three key moments in the novel as a whole. Under each one, write a suitable quotation and one or two key words that sum up the significance of the moment in terms of the main themes. Instead of words, you might prefer to draw your own icons or symbols under each illustration.

? On a blank sheet of paper write across the page, or draw, other key moments in the novel and label them in a similar way.

? The following questions refer to various characters at random moments in the story. Test your recall by trying to identify the character referred to. With a friend, make up your own questions and test one another. You might like to suggest to your teacher a class quiz on the novel based on these lines:

- Who preferred reading writers like De Foe (Defoe) and Goldsmith to mathematical textbooks by Euclid and others? (Book 1, Chapter 8)

- Who wants to use 1000 barrels of gunpowder to explode all the facts and figures in the world? (Book 1, Chapter 8)

- Who knew more about the life of insects than the life of working people in Coketown? (Book 2, Chapter 6)

- Who was likely to prove that the Good Samaritan was a bad economist? (Book 2, Chapter 12)

- Who went *staggering over the universe with his rusty stiff-legged compasses*? (Book 2, Chapter 12)

? Below is a list of titles that Dickens considered for this novel. Circle in one colour those that you think would have been appropriate. Use another colour for those that you think Dickens sensibly rejected. Discuss with a partner how well each fits.

Prove it!

Stubborn Things

Mr Gradgrind's Facts

The Grindstone

Hard Times

Two and Two are Four

Something Tangible

Our Hard-Headed Friend

Rust and Dust

Simple Arithmetic

A Matter of Calculation

A Mere Question of Figures

The Gradgrind Philosophy

Fact

Hard Heads and Soft Hearts

The True Grinder

Heads and Tales

Black and White

Extremes Meet

Answers to test sections

CH. 3 (P. 30)

1e, 2c, 3b, 4d, 5a

CH. 6 (P. 37)

(a) Bounderby, **(b)** elephant, **(c)** Sissy at Bounderby, **(d)** a member of Sleary's circus.

END OF BOOK THE FIRST (P. 55)

(1) Sleary, **(2)** Gradgrind, **(3)** Rachel, **(4)** Bounderby.

Literary critics have written about their responses to *Hard Times* and arrived at different conclusions, some positive and some negative and some trying to steer a middle course.

When the novel was first published it was criticized in *The Rambler* as a book where *character is caricature, sentiment tinsel, and moral (if any) unsound*. A more modern criticism points to the binary opposition between *fact*, as exemplified by Gradgrind's school and Bounderby's factory, and *fancy*, as represented by Sleary's circus, and argues that it is all too systematic for its own good. The critic John Lucas writes about the novel being *in the grip of an idea* and a general criticism is that this has led to a novel that is too **didactic**, meaning it sets out to instruct, and too **polemical**, meaning it involves itself in a controversial discussion. David Lodge (see 'Further reading', below), on the other hand, argues that the rhetoric and polemicism usually work very successfully and only occasionally are there failures.

Lodge identifies *Hard Times* as a polemical novel, attacking contemporary society by way of the contemporary Utilitarian philosophy which impoverishes the educational system and produces emotionally and morally weak individuals. This theme is related to a broader political canvas by showing such individuals growing into victims of an industrial society that may be materially successful but which is as impoverished as the school system in moral and spiritual terms. Lodge sees the social and political criticism of Dickens as radically extending to two major forces for possible reform of society: parliamentary reform through legislation and trade union organization. Neither is seen to offer much hope and Dickens is seen to put his faith in a change of the human heart and the power of human relationships to sustain society in a state of altruistic anarchy. This is seen as a weakness in the novel but nevertheless it is judged as a successful polemical work of art.

The opening descriptions of Gradgrind and Bounderby, and the way in which Coketown becomes a metaphor for the quality of life it offers its inhabitants, are discussed by Lodge as positive examples of the way in which Dickens uses language to

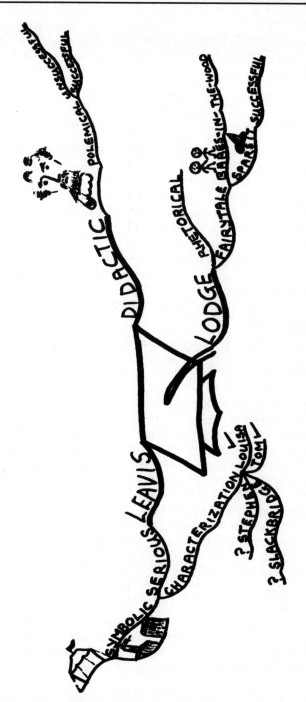

express a vision of his society. Lodge sees Slackbridge as a failure of characterization because the rhetorical style fails: *we miss the metaphorical inventiveness* that distinguishes most of the other descriptions of people. We are told, bluntly, what kind of a man Slackbridge is instead of coming to see the kind of man he is through the language and style.

An interesting aspect of Lodge's essay on *Hard Times* is his discussion of the 'fairy-tale' element in the novel. Louisa and Tom can be seen as the Babes in the Wood who are fenced about with dangers, with Louisa later becoming the enchanted princess with an ice-cold heart, Mrs Pegler as the mysterious old woman and Mrs Sparsit as the evil witch. The description of Mrs Sparsit in the thunderstorm (Book 2, Chapter 10) is quoted as a convincing example of this. Lodge makes the point that these fairytale elements are used successfully as a rhetorical device to express the injustice and impoverishment of a materialistic society. When Sissy becomes the good fairy who confronts and dismisses Harthouse the rhetoric is seen to fail because it depends purely on the idea of the good fairy triumphing over evil.

A very positive response to *Hard Times* was registered by F.R. Leavis' essay which first appeared in *Scrutiny*, a periodical of critical essays, in 1947, before being reprinted as an appendix to his *The Great Tradition*. Leavis calls the novel a *masterpiece ... completely serious* and a *moral fable*. The novel's status and function as a moral fable explains its intensity of meaning, so that every aspect of character and action contributes to its central moral message. Social criticism, Leavis points out, always found a place in a Dickens novel but in *Hard Times* it moves from the periphery to the centre and his society becomes the focus of a searching and coherent critique. *What Gradgrind stands for is, though repellent, nevertheless respectable*, for it underpins the *free market* economic philosophy that judged people like Bounderby a success.

Leavis praises Dickens for the depth and sustained consistency of his critical vision and shows how Sissy, for example, resists the narrow diet of her education for a healthier sense of humanity. She takes on a rich symbolic meaning that expresses itself through images, like the one from Chapter 11 where the ray of light coming through the schoolroom's window illuminates Sissy while emphasizing Bitzer's deficiency of vitality at the same time. Her essential goodness takes on a moral force that subverts the *calculating self-interest* of Victorian society.

Leavis himself raises the possible objection that while Coketown has a material reality that emerges from the fiction, the same cannot be said about the symbolic meaning that Dickens invests in horse-riding. It could instead be unrealistic and sentimental because horse-riding could not have been so charged with goodness as the novel makes it. Leavis defends the approach on the grounds that such goodness does exist and the author chose the circus as a metaphor for this fact. He creates a diverse set of characters, including the alcohol-prone, *flabby-surfaced* Mr Sleary, who is hardly an ideal creation. A lack of realism is detected in Stephen Blackpool, who is too good, and Slackbridge, who is a caricature trade unionist, but not in Sissy, Louisa or Tom. The emotional poverty of Louisa's early years encourages her to transfer her feelings to Tom's welfare and her fleeing to her father is praised as a scene of power and conviction. Gradgrind is a human figure and the turmoil in his daughter brings him anguish as his system collapses around him. By way of dramatic contrast, the revelation of Tom's character to Gradgrind is handled in a tone of high comedy, grim and sardonic.

Above all, Leavis praises Dickens' mastery of language and controlled inventiveness. His style conveys meaning in a word or an image and he brings an emotional strength to scenes through an exemplary sense of theatre. Mrs Gradgrind's death is quoted as an example of the skill with which Dickens moves between the narrative voice and the direct speech. The essay concludes by saying that this scene is an example of Dickens' achievement as a dramatic artist and as a realist operating in a highly imaginative mode of fiction.

FURTHER READING

Peter Ackroyd, *Dickens* (Minerva, 1990). Chapter 23 of this biography covers the writing of *Hard Times*.

F. R. Leavis, *The Great Tradition* (London, 1955).

David Lodge, *Language of Fiction* (Routledge & Kegan Paul, 1966). An essay on 'The Rhetoric of *Hard Times*'.

HOW TO GET AN 'A' IN ENGLISH LITERATURE

In *all your study, in coursework, and in exams, be aware of the following:*

- **Characterization** – the characters and how we know about them (e.g. speech, actions, author description), their relationships, and how they develop.
- **Plot and structure** – the story and how it is organized into parts or episodes.
- **Setting and atmosphere** – the changing physical scene and how it reflects the story (e.g. a storm reflecting chaos).
- **Style and language** – the author's choice of words, and literary devices such as imagery, and how these reflect the **mood**.
- **Viewpoint** – how the story is told (e.g. through an imaginary narrator, or in the third person but through the eyes of one character – 'She was furious – how dare he!').
- **Social and historical context** – the author's influences (see 'Context').
- **Critical approaches** – different ways in which the text has been, or could be, interpreted.

Develop *your ability to:*

- Relate **detail** to **broader content, meaning and style**.
- Show understanding of the author's **intentions, technique and meaning** (brief and appropriate comparisons with other works by the same author will gain marks).
- Give **personal response and interpretation**, backed up by **examples** and short **quotations**.
- **Evaluate** the author's achievement (how far does he/she succeed – give reasons).

Make *sure you:*

- Use **paragraphs** and **sentences** correctly.
- Write in an appropriate **register** – formal but not stilted.
- Use short, appropriate quotations as **evidence** of your understanding.
- Use **literary terms** correctly to explain how an author achieves effects.

Planning

You will probably have about 45 minutes for one essay. It is worth spending about 5–10 minutes planning it. An excellent way to do this is in the three stages below.

1 **Mind Map** your ideas, without worrying about their order yet.
2 **Order** the relevant ideas (the ones that really relate to the question) by numbering them in the order in which you will write the essay.
3 **Gather** your evidence and short quotations.

You could remember this as the **MOG** technique.

Writing and checking

Then write the essay, allowing five minutes at the end for checking relevance, spelling, grammar and punctuation.

Remember!

Stick to the question, and always **back up** your points with evidence – examples and short quotations. Note: you can use '…' for unimportant words missed out in a quotation.

Model answer and plan

The next (and final) chapter consists of an answer to an exam question on *Hard Times*, with the Mind Map and plan used to write it. Don't be put off if you think you couldn't write an essay like this yet. You'll develop your skills if you work at them. Even if you're reading this the night before the exam, you can easily memorize the MOG technique in order to do your personal best.

The model answer and plan are good examples to follow, but don't learn them by heart. It's better to pay close attention to the wording of the question you choose to answer, and allow Mind Mapping to help you to think creatively and structurally.

Before reading the answer, you might like to do a plan of your own to compare with the example. The numbered points, with comments at the end, show why it's a good answer.

QUESTION

Hard Times has been criticized for being too schematic and simplistic. How far do you agree with this view of the novel?

PLAN

- General response to the question showing an understanding of the terms.
- Acknowledge the potential force of the criticism and extent of its validity.
- Explain how the novel succeeds as a complex whole.
- Non-simplistic characterizations of Louisa and Tom.
- Complexity of the novel's conclusion.
- Conclusion, summing up response to essay title.

ESSAY

There is no denying the schematic nature of *Hard Times*, which makes itself felt in the structure, the style and the thematic meaning of the novel. It is not so obvious that it is too schematic and the related criticism, with the implication that the application of a scheme or plan lacking complexity and subtlety leads to a simplistic novel, is not accepted.[1]

The underlying scheme that structures and gives meaning to the novel is the opposition between a narrow rationalism, as represented primarily by Gradgrind, and an imaginative capacity exemplified by the world of the circus and Sissy in particular. It is true that this opposition goes to the heart of the novel and if the scheme is seen to be handled in a crude or shallow way then indeed *Hard Times* is open to the charge of being simplistic. The rhetorical style of the novel constantly draws our attention to this underlying conflict between reason and the imagination and it is announced insistently in the opening chapters of the book. This central theme runs through the novel and the conclusion to the plot, with the defeat of Bitzer's attempt to arrest Tom with the help of the circus folk, can be seen as the triumph of imagination over reason.

If this level of analysis is maintained then the novel is reduced to a simplistic scheme and the criticism holds true. What it leaves out, however, is the role of language, characterization and style, which make the treatment of the central theme rich, complex and convincing. There are occasional lapses, such as the characterization of Slackbridge, and to a lesser extent Stephen Blackpool, but these do not weaken the success of the novel as a whole.[2]

In the first chapter of the book the language and rhetoric are carefully controlled so as to gain the reader's involvement in the central theme about to unfold. Characterization succeeds with Gradgrind and Bounderby because of the way the language works metaphorically and details accumulate, such as the way their houses take on their personalities. Slackbridge fails as a character because he is not evoked through metaphor or a flight of fancy and we are merely told what kind of a person he is. The language fails, in other words, and in doing so reveals Dickens' own ambivalence towards trade unions.

What adds depth to the central theme, however, is the way the gradual disintegration of the Gradgrind family plays out, at a very human level, what is wrong with society's values. Mrs Gradgrind's enigmatic observation that *there's a pain somewhere in the room … but I couldn't positively say that I have got it* brings us to the heart of Gradgrind's inadequacy as a parent and the hollowness of his rationalist philosophy. In her dying moments, Mrs Gradgrind speaks of *something, not an Ology at all – that your father has missed* and it is left to the reader to ponder and reflect on this. Dickens is writing a polemical novel, with clearly directed social criticism, but it is not propaganda and it is not simplistic.[3]

The characterization of Louisa is one of the strongest in the novel and it counters any charge of over-schematization. As F.R. Leavis argues, the emotional poverty of her childhood explains the concentration of her feelings on Tom's welfare, and her desperate escape to her father is rendered powerful and moving. Gradgrind, who began as a caricature, develops into a human figure whose inner turmoil comes to the surface as his system collapses, literally, around him: *And he laid her down there, and saw the pride of his heart and the triumph of his system, lying an insensible heap, at his feet.* Dickens changes the tone to one of high comedy and sardonic humour in the scene where Tom's character is revealed to his father. His fanciful escape, disguised as a black servant and then a country buffoon, carries a symbolic power that completes the demolition of those values his father exemplified.[4]

The novel's conclusion, in particular, refutes the argument that the novel is too schematic and one-dimensional. Gradgrind is a changed person but the values he once held have not disappeared and there is no simplistic, fairytale conclusion. Coketown is still there and Bounderby may have been exposed but his economic and social power remains intact. Bitzer is promoted and twenty-five new Bounderbys are cloned in his will, with all that it implies. Mrs Sparsit may have been sent packing but the social divisiveness she so grotesquely represented remains to wreak its harm. It is left to Sissy to hold out a vision of private happiness and Dickens can only ask his readers to follow her example.[5]

There is a discernible scheme to *Hard Times* but it is realized in a complex way, combining psychologically convincing characters with a language rich in metaphor and symbolic force. The serious social and political issues that are explored in the novel are not rendered in a simplistic manner and, despite the occasional weakness, the author's vision is a powerful, persuasive and disturbing one.[6]

WHAT EARNED THE MARKS?

1 Concise introduction, focusing on the question, showing an understanding of the key terms and summarizing the response which the essay will go on to develop.

2 Setting out the terms by which the criticism can be judged,

acknowledging weaknesses but pointing to the way the essay will reject the criticism.

3 Examples and quotations to support a positive reading of the novel that counters the criticism.

4 Further examples, focusing on characterization, to support the point of view, and a reference to a literary critic.

5 Analysis of the novel's conclusion to refute the criticism in the essay's title.

6 Clear conclusion that returns to the essay title.

It is very important to realize that the above essay does not represent the only way of successfully dealing with the essay title. It would be an extreme position to adopt without some qualifications, but in theory it would be legitimate to agree with the criticism and then go on to develop this position. Such an approach would need to address and deal with the positive points that are made above in this model essay. For example, you would need to address the characterization of Louisa and the novel's conclusion and argue that they fit the charge of being too schematic and simplistic.

This might be difficult but, nevertheless, there is plenty of scope to choose other aspects of the novel to discuss and to arrive at a conclusion that offers a different balance to the one adopted here. For example, there is the criticism that the symbolic meaning invested in the circus is unconvincing, unrealistic and sentimental. Having said that, this criticism can be countered along the lines that Leavis adopts, defending the approach on the grounds that such goodness does exist and the author chose the circus as a metaphor for this fact.

What is important, and what examiners will reward with high marks, is a clearly structured essay, hence the value of drawing, however quickly, a Mini Mind Map in response to the essay title. Examiners are also looking for an essay that deals explicitly with the terms of the essay title and which argues its case with reference to the text and with a good understanding of the issues relevant to the question being asked.

GLOSSARY OF LITERARY TERMS

alliteration   the repetition, for effect, of consonant sounds.

allusion   the use of literary, cultural and historical references.

assonance   the repetition, for effect, of vowel sounds.

caricature   exaggeration and simplification of character traits.

characterization   the way in which characters are presented.

context   the background of social, historical and literary influences on a work.

dialect   regional form of language varying from the standard in vocabulary and grammar.

diction   choice and arrangement of words.

didactic   intended to instruct; in literary criticism, often used in negative sense.

discursive   presenting a logical argument, step by step.

epistolary novel   genre of fiction in which the plot unfolds through letters.

feminist criticism   critical approach developed in the 1960s, based on assessing the role of gender in texts. A particular issue is the subordination of women in a patriarchal society.

film noir   genre of film accentuating menace and foreboding.

free indirect speech   technique of blending a character's words and thoughts with those of the narrator.

genre   type of literary work conforming to certain expectations; e.g. tragedy.

Gothic novel   genre of fiction popular in the eighteenth century, in which eerie and supernatural events take place in sinister settings.

idiom   a characteristic expression of a language or ***dialect.***

image   a word picture bringing an idea to life by appealing to the senses.

industrial novel   novel dealing with the issues of the Industrial Revolution, often set in the north of England; e.g. *North and South* by Elizabeth Gaskell.

irony   a style of writing in which one thing is said and another is meant, used for a variety of effects, such as criticism or ridicule.

magical realism   a fiction style which combines mythical elements, bizarre events and a strong sense of cultural tradition; e.g. *Midnight's Children* by Salman Rushdie.

Marxist criticism   critical approach which sees literature in relation to class struggle, and assesses the way texts present social realities.

melodrama   sensational dramatic piece appealing to the emotions, usually ending happily.

metaphor   a compressed *simile* describing something as if it were something else.

narrator   in a novel, a character who tells the story. An *omniscient* narrator has complete knowledge of everything that takes place in the narrative; an *unreliable* narrator is one whose knowledge and judgements are limited and biased.

onomatopoeia   use of words whose sound imitates the thing they describe.

paradox   an apparently contradictory statement which contains some truth; e.g. 'I hear her hair has turned quite gold from grief' (*The Importance of Being Earnest*).

parody   an exaggerated copy (especially of a writer's style) made for humorous effect.

persona   an assumed identity.

personification   an *image* speaking of something abstract, such as love, death or sleep, as if it were a person or a god.

picaresque   type of novel popular in the eighteenth century, featuring the adventures of a wandering rogue; e.g. *Tom Jones* by Henry Fielding.

plot   the story; the events that take place and how they are arranged.

polemical   (of style) making an argument.

rhetorical   expressed with a view to persuade (often used in negative sense).

satire   literature which humorously exposes and ridicules vice and folly.

signifiers   verbal signs.

simile an *image*   comparing two things similar in some way but different in others, normally using 'like' or 'as'.

standard English   the particular form of English, originally based on East Midlands dialect, most often used by educated speakers in formal situations.

stream of consciousness   technique exploring the thought processes and unconscious minds of characters; used by writers such as Virginia Woolf and James Joyce.

structure   the organization of a text; e.g. narrative, plot, repeated images and symbols.

subplot   subsidiary plot coinciding with the main plot and often reflecting aspects of it.

tone   the mood created by a writer's choice and organization of words; e.g. persuasive.

viewpoint   the way a narrator approaches the material and the audience.

INDEX

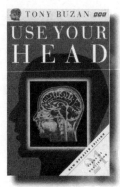

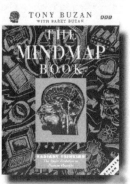